Realizing the Power
of Professional Learning

Heidi —
You're an amazing leader!
girl! We will miss you.
Lisa et al. :)

Realizing the Power of Professional Learning

Helen S. Timperley

 Open University Press

Open University Press
McGraw-Hill Education
McGraw-Hill House
Shoppenhangers Road
Maidenhead
Berkshire
England
SL6 2QL

email: enquiries@openup.co.uk
world wide web: www.openup.co.uk

and Two Penn Plaza, New York, NY 10121-2289, USA

First published 2011

A catalogue record of this book is available from the British Library

ISBN-13: 978 0 335 24404 1 (pb)   978 0 335 24403 4 (hb)
ISBN-10: 0 335 22404 1 (pb)   0 335 24403 3 (hb)
eISBN: 978 0 335 24405 8

Library of Congress Cataloging-in-Publication Data
CIP data applied for

Typeset by RefineCatch Limited, Bungay, Suffolk
Printed and bound by CPI Group (UK) Ltd, Croydon, CR0 4YY

Fictitious names of companies, products, people, characters and/or data
that may be used herein (in case studies or in examples) are not intended
to represent any real individual, company, product or event.

The *McGraw·Hill* Companies

Contents

CONTENTS

Series Editors' introduction

Expanding Educational Horizons

In confronting the many challenges that the future holds in store, humankind sees in education an indispensable asset ...

(Jaques Delors et al.[1])

The dizzying speed of the modern world puts education at the heart of both personal and community development; its mission is to enable everyone, without exception, to develop all their talents to the full and to realize their creative potential, including responsibility for their own lives and achievement of their personal aims.

Education, unfortunately, does not always keep up with the times. Sometimes it appears to be moving in step with changes; at other times it still seems to be in the past century. Many years of research have shown us that tinkering around the edges of schooling will not help educators meet the challenges that children and young people will face in their future. Current interventions are having limited effects.[2,3] Even if levels of attainment are getting better, the gap in educational achievement between the most and least advantaged is far too wide in many places. Every child and young person has to be well equipped to seize learning opportunities throughout life, to broaden her or his knowledge, skills and attitudes, and to be able to adapt to a changing, complex and interconnected world[4]. It is possible to maximize the opportunity of achieving 'preferred futures'[5] for children and young people, for the teaching profession, and for schools. But what is required is a bold and imaginative reorientation to educational purposes, policies and practices.

In this series, we want to provide a forum for suggesting and thinking about different and more powerful ways of ensuring that all students are prepared to take an active and proactive role in their future, that all teachers and other adults are best able to help them learn effectively, that all leaders and community members can rise to the challenges of ensuring that nothing stands in their way, and that learning environments are designed in such a way to ensure this high level learning and success for all students. We believe it is time to expand educational horizons.

Authors in this international series provide fresh views on things we take for granted and alternative ways of addressing educational challenges. Exploring trends, ideas, current and emerging developments and professional learning needs, they offer a variety of perspectives of what education could be; not what it has been or, even, is. The books are designed to engage your imagination, to inform, to encourage you to 'look beyond' and help others to do so, to challenge thinking, to inspire, to motivate, to promote deep reflection, collaboration and thoughtful action, to stimulate learning and deep change; and to offer avenues of action and concrete possibilities.

We hope that the series will appeal to a wide audience of practitioners, local authority/district personnel, professional developers, policy makers and applied academics working in a variety of different contexts and countries. Primarily, we are looking to support and challenge busy professionals working in education who do not always feel they have time to read books. The research on professional learning that makes a difference is clear: educators need the stimulus of external ideas.[6,7] The books are intended for use by people in schools/colleges, local authorities/districts, consultants; national, state and regional policy makers; and professional developers; for example, those involved in leadership development. They will be valuable for people involved in ongoing professional learning programmes. They may also be important additions to Masters' courses that are geared to investigating practice as it is and as it might be.

The books are deliberately relatively short, laid out in a way that we hope will add to readability, and contain practical suggestions for action, questions for reflection and to stimulate learning conversations, highlighted quotes and suggested follow-up reading. Each book can be read as a stand alone, but the focus on looking beyond what is to what might be is the linking feature, and each book has a broadly similar format, to facilitate the connections.

In this book, *Realizing the Power of Professional Learning*, Helen Timperley takes us inside a world that is both comfortably familiar and unsettlingly original. Her exploration of the concept of professional learning moves us far beyond long-standing notions of professional development in which teachers sit and receive, to a view of professional learning as an internal process that requires active cognitive, emotional and practical engagement as teachers create professional knowledge in a way that challenges previous assumptions and creates new meanings. She draws on compelling evidence from her own research and development activities to describe a cycle of inquiry that has students as the touchstone and is focused on building professional knowledge and improvements in practice to meet the needs of students in more powerful ways. The collaborative inquiry cycle applies not only to teacher learning but to learning for leaders and for others who are interested in supporting deep change in classroom practice that influences student learning. As Timperley describes it, the process is deceptively simple. The challenge is for educators everywhere to expect and to look forward to engaging in constant learning and reflection, as a routine part of their daily work. What could be more exciting?

Louise Stoll and Lorna Earl

References

1 Delors, J., Al Mufti, I., Amagi, A., Carneiro, R., Chung, F., Geremek, B., Gorham, W., Kornhauser, A., Manley, M., Padrón Quero, M., Savané, M-A., Singh, K., Stavenhagen, R., Suhr, M.W. and Nanzhao, Z. (1996) *Learning: The Treasure Within – Report to UNESCO of the International Commission on Education for the Twenty-first Century.* Paris: UNESCO.

2 Coburn, S. (2003) Rethinking scale: moving beyond numbers to deep and lasting change, *Educational Researcher*, 32(6): 3–12.

3 Elmore, R. (2004) *School Reform from the Inside Out: Policy, Practice and Performance.* Cambridge, MA: Harvard Education Press.

4 Delors, J., Al Mufti, I., Amagi, A., Carneiro, R., Chung, F., Geremek, B., Gorham, W., Kornhauser, A., Manley, M., Padrón Quero, M., Savané,

M-A., Singh, K., Stavenhagen, R., Suhr, M.W. and Nanzhao, Z. (1996) *Learning: The Treasure Within – Report to UNESCO of the International Commission on Education for the Twenty-first Century.* Paris: UNESCO.

5 Beare, H. (2001) *Creating the Future School.* London: RoutledgeFalmer.
6 Cordingley, P., Bell, M., Isham, C., Evans, D. and Fifth, A. (2007) What do specialists do in CPD programmes for which there is evidence of positive outcomes for pupil and teachers? Report, in *Research Evidence in Education Library.* London: EPPI-Centre, Social Science Research Unit, Institute of Education, University of London.
7 Timperley, H., Wilson, A., Barrar, H. and Fung, I. (2008) *Teacher Professional Learning and Development: Best Evidence Synthesis Iteration.* New Zealand: Ministry of Education.

Preface

This book is the culmination of an extended research and development programme over more than 10 years. The origins of this programme involved curiosity about what teachers need to learn, and the conditions under which they learn it, in order to make a difference to student outcomes that are valued by the communities in which the students live and are educated. As I have worked on this issue it has become apparent that focusing on teachers and their learning is not enough. School leaders and others in the system involved in professional learning also need to learn and change in very specific ways if teacher learning is to result in the kind of system lift that 'raises the bar and closes the gap for all students'.

My research and development programme has three strands. One is theoretical in the sense of understanding how teachers learn and why some approaches to professional learning might be better than others. One important question with respect to this strand asks whether the processes of professional learning are fundamentally different from the processes for student learning. My response is that they are very similar. Clearly, teachers bring far richer knowledge and skills to the learning context, but the processes by which they learn new knowledge and skills are little different from their younger student counterparts. Two committees within the National Research Council in the United States[1] identified some key processes through which people learn. In brief, the first involves engaging learners' prior conceptions of how the world works. The second is the need to develop a deep foundation of factual knowledge that is understood within conceptual frameworks. The third is the development of meta-cognitive awareness so learners are able to take control of their own learning. The worth of these findings in informing my work about professional learning has proved invaluable.

The second strand is a synthesis of the empirical literature about the kinds of professional learning and development associated with positive outcomes for students' engagement, learning and well-being.[2] The synthesis included both primary and secondary schools and threw up some surprising findings. As one example, the evidence fails to show that teachers who volunteer to participate in professional development are more likely to make the kinds of changes that result in better outcomes for students than those who participate more reluctantly. It appears few teachers expect to change much as a result of their participation, whether they volunteer or not. What is more important than initial volunteering is their level of engagement over time. Another example is that there was little difference in the emphasis or processes for the kinds of teacher learning that made a difference to students in primary and secondary schools. In academic areas, both groups needed to learn about the curriculum, how to teach it and how to assess it.

As I was reading and thinking about the meaning of the theoretical and empirical literature for the synthesis, I was also co-leading a research and development project alongside a national professional development initiative in literacy. This project has involved over 300 primary schools in New Zealand participating in groups of 100 over two years. Many of the findings emerging from the synthesis were used to inform and solve the problems that became evident through the research within the project. Thus an iterative process was developed in which the theoretical and empirical work of the synthesis was trialled in practice and what emerged from practice influenced my thinking about the synthesis. At the same time colleagues in other parts of the world were using the findings in exciting ways in their work and contributed their ideas.

This combination of theory, evidence and trialling in practice has led to some important understandings about effective teacher professional learning and development and challenges many of the assumptions underpinning current approaches to professional development. In this book I detail these understandings and translate them into the complexities of teaching and leadership practice.

One important understanding relates to how teachers think about their students. Those who believe that their students have some level of fixed innate intelligence have little reason to undertake a serious search for ways to make their teaching more meaningful to those who do not share their backgrounds and so do not understand them as readily as others. On the other hand, those teachers who realize that being smart is something that is essentially learned have more compelling reasons to engage. In the first book in this series on new kinds of smart, Bill Lucas and Guy Claxton[3] describe how intelligence is made up of a number of complex attributes that are shaped by learning. Teachers who actively cultivate new kinds of smart for both themselves and their students have demonstrated dramatic successes with teaching the diversity of students for whom they have responsibility for educating.

A second and related understanding is that professional learning requires active cognitive, emotional and practical engagement from teachers. The knowledge and skills needed to make the transformational changes for students are not those that teachers can just sit and receive. Yet these approaches underpin many of the traditional approaches to professional development. Teachers have long complained of being 'done to' by those who claim they know more than the teachers themselves. But leaving teachers to it does not lead to transformational changes to practice either. Processes for active inquiry, learning and experimenting have to become teachers' core business of thinking as a professional.

Such a demanding learning agenda immediately raises issues of motivation. How can school leaders persuade reluctant teachers to engage in this more intense level of learning? In one study I led, we found that teachers' motivation increased when their students showed accelerated progress.[4] The best evidence synthesis identified that the more student achievement improved, the more motivated the teachers became. Improved student engagement, learning and well-being must form the reason for teachers to engage, the reason for them to keep going, and the basis for judging if they are successful. Even small changes in students' responses to new approaches to teaching can improve teacher motivation.

These kinds of change also challenge the roles and responsibilities of school leaders, professional learning facilitators and policy officials. Teachers cannot achieve this level of learning and change alone. The context in which they work strongly influences what and how they learn. Leaders cannot stand aloof from the professional learning agenda. Rather, an effective process usually becomes as challenging for them as it is for the teachers.

Part of the leaders' learning agenda is to assess rather than to assume that simply because something has been changed that it is more effective than what was done before. Steven Katz and colleagues[5] alert us to the dangers of activity traps, that is, 'those "doings" that, while well intentioned, are not truly needs based and have the effect of diverting resources (both human and material) away from where they are most necessary'. Avoiding activity traps requires constant checking of the effectiveness of changes made on a daily, weekly and extended time basis. Educating children, their teachers and leaders is full of uncertainties. The uncertainties mean that there are no context-free understandings or practices that can be guaranteed to result in the desired outcomes. Systems for checking the effectiveness of change are central to ongoing improvement. A focus on inputs and distant outcomes, such as changes to student achievement alone, needs to shift to identifying what is believed to lead to what and testing whether everyone's efforts are heading in the right direction while they are happening, not in some far-off future.

This book

This book combines theory, evidence and practical examples using real cases from my work and that of my colleagues. The introductory chapter begins by outlining concerns about the lack of impact of current professional development provision and describes the shifts in thinking required to address those concerns. It introduces a cycle of inquiry that has students as the touchstone and is focused on building professional knowledge and improvements in practice to better meet the needs of students. Each part of the cycle is described briefly together with the implications for leadership.

Chapter 2 begins with the first dimension of the inquiry and knowledge-building cycle that asks about students. For professional learning opportunities to result in better outcomes for students, the primary purpose for engagement must be to enhance those outcomes that are valued by the community within which the students live and learn. The guiding question for this chapter asks 'What knowledge and skills do our students need to meet curricula and other goals?'

Chapter 3 moves to the second and third dimensions of the inquiry and knowledge-building cycle with a focus on identifying and building teachers' knowledge. It examines the kinds of knowledge and skills needed if teachers are to address their students' learning needs. The guiding question for this chapter asks, 'What knowledge and skills do we as professionals need to meet the learning needs of our students?' If teachers can be assisted to answer this question, they are able to take control of their own learning agenda and ensure that the support they receive meets their learning needs. Motivation to engage typically rises rather than falls under such circumstances.

Chapter 4 moves to the fourth and fifth dimensions of the inquiry cycle with a focus on checking the impact of changes made. The first check involves changes to teaching practices. If nothing changes in classrooms, little is likely to happen for students. The second check involves changes to those student outcomes identified as needing attention in the first dimension of the inquiry cycle. These checks should also include any unintended consequences in case solving one problem creates problems in other areas.

Chapter 5 shifts the focus from teachers to school leadership. It is too difficult for teachers on their own to achieve sustained changes to outcomes for students. In a synthesis of the empirical literature linking leadership practices to student learning, Viviane Robinson and colleagues[6] identified that leaders who promoted and participated in teacher professional development had the greatest gains in student achievement. Given the robustness of these findings and the evidence from my research, this chapter uses the analogy of leaders as teachers of 'their class' of professionals. The essence of their job is promoting the learning of their class. The composition of that class depends on the size of the school and the designated leadership positions.

Chapter 6 brings the material from the earlier chapters together and illustrates through two extended cases how the different dimensions of the inquiry and knowledge-building cycle apply in very different professional learning situations. One case describes how the staff in a secondary school undertook an inquiry into how they could be more successful in developing independent inquiry and reflection in senior students. The other case takes a more micro-process perspective and identifies how coaching through the observation and analysis of teaching practice can deepen teachers' learning. Improved outcomes for students on challenging content have resulted in both cases.

Chapter 7 shifts the leadership focus to those external to the school who facilitate professional learning in schools. They are variously referred to as in-service or professional development providers, consultants, teacher educators or facilitators of professional learning. Sometimes they are head teachers (principals) from other schools taking responsibility for the learning of their colleagues. In the same way that within-school leaders need to know 'their class', so must those with external roles. Their class may be the school leadership team so they can, in turn, become more skilled in working with their class of teachers. The class may comprise a network of school principals. This chapter identifies the kinds of knowledge and skills these facilitators of professional learning must have to be able to take on this complex role.

The final chapter brings together influences on maintaining momentum over the longer term in ways that lead to increasing effectiveness of practice and sustained gains for students. One influence involves embedding the inquiry and knowledge-building processes into the 'core' business of schools. Another is the importance of establishing coherence across teaching processes, new initiatives, and professional learning plans for teachers. Shifting from one idea to the next, no matter how good, usually results in superficial learning and/or teacher burnout. Coherence means planning how all school and professional learning activities contribute to common and agreed goals. The final influence looks outside the school and discusses the role of policy officials in promoting conditions that facilitate teacher learning.

Each chapter ends by identifying three practices that are central to the success of professional learning. Each of these practices is followed by descriptions of what they might look like at basic, developing and integrated levels. The reader is invited to decide which of the descriptions most closely fits their current situation and what they might need to do for their practice to shift to the more integrated end of the continuum. This activity is based on research about the kinds of tools and routines that are effective in promoting professional learning.[7]

References

1 Committee on Developments in the Science of Learning: Bransford, J., Brown, A. and Cocking, R. (eds) and Committee on Learning Research and Educational Practice: Donovan, S., Bransford, J. and Pellegrino, J. (eds) (2000) *How People Learn: Brain, Mind, Experience and School.* Washington, DC: National Academy Press.

2 Timperley, H., Wilson, A., Barrar, H. and Fung, I. (2008) Best evidence synthesis on professional learning and development. Report to the Ministry of Education, Wellington, New Zealand.

3 Lucas, B. and Claxton, G. (2010) *New Kinds of Smart: How the Science of Learnable Intelligence is Changing Education.* Maidenhead: Open University Press.

4 Timperley, H.S. and Phillips, G. (2003) Changing and sustaining teachers' expectations through professional development in literacy, *Journal of Teaching and Teacher Education*, 19: 627–41.

5 Katz, S., Earl, L. and Ben Jafaar, S. (2009) *Building and Connecting Learning Communities: The Power of Networks for School Improvement* (p. 24). Thousand Oaks, CA: Corwin Press.

6 Robinson, V.M.J., Lloyd, C. and Rowe, K.J. (2008) The impact of leadership on student outcomes: an analysis of the differential effects of leadership type, *Educational Administration Quarterly*, 44(5): 635–74.

7 Timperley, H. and Parr, J. (2009) Chain of influence from policy to practice in the New Zealand literacy strategy, *Research Papers in Education*, 24(2): 135–54.

Acknowledgements

Books like this that are based on an extended research and development programme do not happen without the involvement of many others in the research and practice underpinning them. I have many research colleagues who have worked alongside me in developing the synthesis and researching the resulting practice. Those primarily involved in a research role have included Professors Judy Parr and Stuart McNaughton, Dr Mei Lai, Aaron Wilson and Heather Barrar.

Equally influential have been those people I worked alongside in a development role and include particularly Dr Pamela O'Connell, Lyn Bareta and Carolyn English from Learning Media Ltd together with the 25 national facilitators who have allowed me to observe their practice and have sent me numerous transcripts of their interactions with school leaders and teachers to analyse. They have all been gracious in receiving feedback and have helped me to work out better ways to do things. Without the school leaders and teachers, of course, I would never have been able to assess the effectiveness of ideas in real contexts.

ACKNOWLEDGEMENTS

I wish also to acknowledge those with whom I have worked in the New Zealand Ministry of Education. I have had the privilege of interacting with many people within the Ministry but those I would like to name in particular include Denise Arnerich and Dr Brian Annan (now at the University of Auckland). They have never acted as faceless bureaucrats, but rather have debated the issues, pointed out where I have bordered on the unrealistic, and commented constructively on my various efforts to understand the chain of influence from policy to practice. Some of the material in the book has arisen from my work in the iterative Best Evidence Synthesis programme so ably led by Dr Adrienne Alton-Lee. At the same time as acknowledging the contribution of these people, I must note that the material presented in this book represents my ideas and not necessarily those of the Ministry of Education.

I am also grateful to my colleagues in the United Kingdom and Canada, particularly Drs Linda Kaser and Judy Halbert who have shared their experiences with me when they have used the material from the synthesis of the literature on professional learning and development, challenged my thinking and provided examples of the amazing things happening in their schools throughout British Columbia.

Robyn Yu has patiently drawn and redrawn diagrams without complaint. Without her help, the chapters would not have her great diagrams.

My final acknowledgement must go to the series editors, Professors Lorna Earl and Louise Stoll, who have provided valuable comment on earlier drafts of this book. Louise has taken me to schools in London and explained the cross-national issues related to their practice. Lorna has done an amazing job in making my academic prose accessible to teachers.

1

From Professional Development to Professional Learning

For far too many teachers ..., staff development is a demeaning, mind numbing experience as they passively 'sit and get'. That staff development is often mandatory in nature ... and evaluated by 'happiness scales'. As one observer put it, 'I hope I die during an in-service session because the transition between life and death would be so subtle'.[1]

Every day teachers and school leaders face new challenges – introducing new curricula, assessment approaches and technologies into their classrooms and schools; serving students who do not respond to teaching practices in familiar ways; ensuring literacy and numeracy for all, and the list goes on. Raising the bar and closing the gap has become a mantra in many countries with teacher professional learning the multi-million dollar solution. Policy directives and billions of dollars, pounds, euros, and so on are being directed into professional development for teachers, with the expectation that this combination will make schools better and improve student learning.

Unfortunately, much of this investment has failed to meet its goals, particularly with respect to improving student learning and engagement. Here is how Larry Cuban[2] summed up the effects of professional development on teachers and teaching over 15 years ago with others[3] echoing this sentiment many times since:

Hurricane winds sweep across the sea tossing up twenty foot waves; a fathom below the surface turbulent waters swirl while on the ocean floor there is unruffled calm.

Many policy makers at the highest levels share these concerns. Eric Hanushek from the International Academy of Education and International Institute for Educational Planning in UNESCO, for example, highlighted the importance of teacher quality while, at the same time, rejected professional development as a key policy lever because *despite some success in general they [professional development programmes] have been disappointing.*[4] The quote from the teacher at the beginning of this chapter shows these sentiments are often shared. Much professional development has little meaning for teachers.

This book is about the kinds of professional learning that does have meaning and makes a difference to student outcomes. In it, I challenge many of the assumptions underpinning traditional approaches to professional learning and offer more effective alternatives – alternatives that actively involve teachers in their learning, are demanding of their professionalism, and have demonstrated improvement in outcomes for students that are valued by the communities in which students learn and live. They are particularly effective for those seemingly intractable problems of low achievement profiles of some groups of students. Tinkering around the edges or leaving teachers to it does not lead to the kinds of change that makes a difference.

> "Tinkering around the edges or leaving teachers to it does not lead to the kinds of change that makes a difference."

The book is based on the *Teacher Professional Learning and Development: Best Evidence Synthesis*[5] I mentioned in the Preface. Over a number of years professional development projects in different parts of the world have found strong evidence of substantial improvements in student achievement. These projects have a number of things in common, many of which come from some fundamental shifts in thinking about professional development, leadership and classroom practice. I have had the privilege of being a researcher attached to one of these successful professional development projects in New Zealand, where professional development facilitators worked with more than 300 primary schools throughout the country in literacy. Students have, on average, made 2.5 to 3.2 times the expected rate of progress in writing and 1.5 and 1.9 times the expected rate of progress in reading over the two years of their schools' involvement. Even more important, the gains have been greatest for the students in the lowest 20 per cent of the achievement band at the beginning of the project. For these students, gains in writing have been five to six times the expected rate of progress and gains in reading more than three times the expected rate.[6] Most schools sustained the rate of gain for new student cohorts for at least three years.[7] Gains for students were the result of some fundamental shifts in thinking about professional development, leadership and classroom practice.

> "Gains for students are the result of some fundamental shifts in thinking about professional development, leadership and classroom practice."

Shifts in thinking about professional learning and development

So, what are these shifts in thinking about professional learning? They are both simple and profound at the same time – moving from professional development to professional learning, focusing on students, attending to requisite knowledge and skills, engaging in systematic inquiry into the effectiveness of practice, being explicit about underpinning theories of professionalism and engaging everyone in the system in learning. The need for these shifts in thinking individually has been identified separately by others. This book expands educational horizons by bringing them together into a conceptual framework that has repeatedly demonstrated its power in promoting the kinds of professional learning that make a difference to students.

> **"**Fundamental shifts in thinking about professional learning involve moving from professional development to professional learning, focusing on students, attending to requisite knowledge and skills, engaging in systematic inquiry into the effectiveness of practice, being explicit about underpinning theories of professionalism and engaging everyone in the system in learning.**"**

From professional development to professional learning

The first shift requires a move from thinking in terms of professional development to thinking in terms of professional learning. Both are intentional, ongoing, systematic processes.[8] Over time, however, the term 'professional development' has taken on connotations of delivery of some kind of information to teachers in order to influence their practice whereas 'professional

4

learning' implies an internal process in which individuals create professional knowledge through interaction with this information in a way that challenges previous assumptions and creates new meanings. Challenge and meaning-making are essential because solving entrenched educational problems requires transformative rather than additive change to teaching practice.

One of the critical differences between the two terms is that professional learning requires teachers to be seriously engaged in their learning whereas professional development is often seen as merely participation. Despite many countries, states and provinces requiring such participation, there is little evidence that it has had an impact on teachers' practices or on student outcomes. If professional learning is the process for solving entrenched education problems for underachieving student populations, it cannot be trivial. It needs to be ongoing and in depth because achieving the kinds of transformational changes required to make the difference will not happen with brief and superficial engagement of teachers. While depth requires time, time should not be taken as a proxy measure for depth. It is entirely possible for groups of teachers to spend considerable time reflecting on their practice with their colleagues while learning little about how to improve student engagement or success.

Students at the centre of professional learning

The second important shift in thinking about professional learning is that students are at the centre of the process. Improvements in student learning and well-being are not a by-product of professional learning but rather its central purpose. Students must be the touchstone and the reason for teachers to engage, the basis for understanding what needs to change and evaluating whether those changes have been effective. Part of this shift involves creating mindsets that have at their core a belief that schooling is about ensuring deep learning for all. Linda Kaser and Judy Halbert[9] remind us that it is no longer acceptable for teachers and leaders to say they provided opportunities for students to learn but *they* did not learn. Having students at the centre means being committed through professional learning to create the conditions where everyone learns including leaders, teachers and students.

Focus on professional knowledge and skills

The third shift in thinking involves foregrounding the knowledge and skills of focus rather than forms or delivery methods of professional learning. The best evidence synthesis on professional learning and development found that a great deal of emphasis was given to descriptions of the details of the activities in which teachers engaged rather than what they learned. No activity or process, whether facilitated by others (e.g. coaching, modelling and engaging with professional readings) or self-directed (e.g. discussing mutually identified problems, reflection and inquiry) was consistently associated with improved student success. What was important? The knowledge and skills learned as a result of engagement in the activity or process.

Often the knowledge and skills that form the focus of professional learning are defined by experts (leaders or researchers) and are not necessarily specific to the immediate demands of classroom teaching and learning. Or, the knowledge and skills presented provide practical suggestions to solve the immediate concerns of this teacher, with these students, from that grade level, without wider reference to theory or principle underlying these suggestions. Neither forms of knowledge are particularly helpful in bringing about sustained improvements in teaching and learning. Generic knowledge, divorced from immediate demands, is likely to be quickly forgotten. On the other hand, knowledge that is specific only to this class of students in this subject area is unlikely to be used with other students or at other times. Rather, the knowledge and skills developed through professional learning must meet the double demand of being both practical and understood in principled ways that can be used to solve teaching and learning challenges encountered in the future.

Professional learning as systematic inquiry

The fourth shift in thinking is about the nature of professional learning that makes a difference. Professional learning is an active process of systematic inquiry into the effectiveness of practice for student engagement, learning and well-being and through this process become self-regulated learners. This inquiry process has many parallels to formative assessment practices found to be effective in promoting student learning. The same processes are applicable to promoting teacher learning. The main difference is that teachers must reference their learning to both themselves and their students. Teachers frame their learning by identifying goals for both; they create partnerships with those with expertise to ensure their learning is focused and achieves desired goals; and they generate information about the pro-gress they are making so that they can monitor and adjust their learning.

Professionalism through reflective inquiry

The fifth shift in thinking is closely related to the fourth. How and what teachers learn must be underpinned by an explicit and defensible theory of professionalism. At the core of decisions about the kinds of knowledge and skills to be promoted is a vision of professionalism that those providing the support hold for the teaching workforce. Walter Doyle[10] contrasted two such views. One portrayed the teacher as a good employee prepared to maintain the prevailing norms of school practices. The approach to professional learning within this view is for teachers to become technicians and learn how to implement the wisdom of others. The alternative view Walter Doyle put forward was the teacher as a reflective professional able to draw on an integrated knowledge base to improve practice through inquiry. Although this vision is underpinned by a more defensible view of professionalism, most approaches based on the reflective practitioner model have not demonstrated a significant impact on important outcomes for students because they have not been explicitly focused on evidence about students. The vision of professionalism promoted in this book requires a shift from the traditional reflective practitioner model to one in which evidence about students, their learning and well-being form the touchstone for teaching and learning in ways that challenge existing assumptions. Through the development of routines that constantly link teaching and student learning, new approaches are sought to solve persistent problems.

Professional learning at all levels

The final shift directs attention to those who support teacher learning within schools or outside of them. Teachers cannot solve entrenched problems within our education system alone, so everyone who has a place in the chain of influence from policy to practice needs to engage in inquiry and knowledge-building cycles to ensure their efforts are effective in developing the kind of professional and student learning that makes a difference. Just like teachers, facilitators of professional learning and school leaders need to engage in ongoing inquiry into the impact of their policies and practices. This impact is not always positive. An important question for all to ask, for example, is whether their approaches to promoting professional learning are consistent with a defensible theory of professionalism. Is the rhetoric about developing motivated professionals who can make informed decisions about their practice based on deep knowledge, then contradicted by approaches to professional learning that involve brief workshops about how to teach something? Michael Fullan[11] suggests that successful problem-solving requires the whole system to be involved in co-dependent partnerships. The research I have undertaken suggests that nowhere is this more important than in the area of professional learning. Successful problem-solving involves a process of learning both up and down the system layers.

Much of the remainder of this chapter and the book unpacks what these shifts mean for teachers and leaders, within schools, local authorities and districts to create the conditions for promoting teachers' professional learning in mutually dependent ways.

Building knowledge through teacher inquiry

Teacher inquiry is not a new idea and is something that many teachers do already. Teachers inquire into the effectiveness of their practice every day as they observe which parts of lessons students appear to understand and what continues to cause them difficulty. Leaders support and assist teachers to inquire through structured opportunities to reflect by reviewing relevant assessment information and considering the effectiveness of practice. This inquiry, however, usually takes place within the frameworks of existing knowledge. If teacher inquiry is going to make a substantive difference to student outcomes, teachers need to be operating within new frameworks and accessing different kinds of knowledge that will push their thinking and challenge their practice. Typically the development of these frameworks and knowledge involve specialist expertise, but not just any expert will do. The quality of this expertise and the ways in which the experts engage with teachers are critical to success.

The best evidence synthesis on professional learning and development identified how cycles of inquiry and knowledge-building can improve students' engagement, learning and well-being (see Figure 1.1). This cycle starts with teachers investigating what students need to know and do to meet goals valued by the communities in which they live and are educated. Students' engagement, learning and well-being are the touchstone. When teachers have a deep understanding of the profiles of their students, they then move to inquire about what knowledge and skills they need if they are to be more effective in addressing the needs of individuals and groups of students, particularly those not achieving as well as others. From there, teachers engage in new professional learning to intentionally deepen their knowledge and refine their professional skills in the focus areas. This new professional learning frames the kinds of new learning experiences that they can bring to their students. But that is not the end. Given that the effectiveness of all teaching practice is influenced by context and no particular practices can be guaranteed to result in particular outcomes, the final stage of the inquiry involves examining the impact of changed

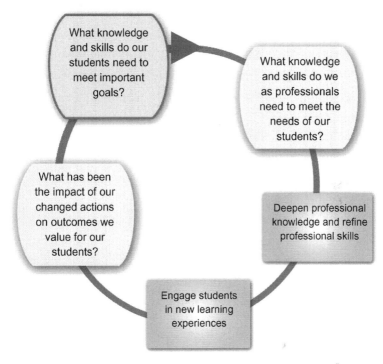

Figure 1.1 Teacher inquiry and knowledge-building cycle to promote important outcomes for students

actions on the outcomes for the students who were the focus of the inquiry. The purpose is to understand what has been effective and what has not. The findings from this examination then lead to another, and usually deeper, cycle of inquiry and knowledge-building. In Figure 1.1, the inquiry questions are in the rounded boxes with the actions often associated with more traditional approaches to professional development identified in the rectangular boxes.

Through engaging in ongoing cycles of inquiry and building knowledge, teachers develop the adaptive expertise required to retrieve, organize and apply professional knowledge when old problems persist or new problems arise. Adaptive expertise can be best understood by contrasting it with routine expertise.[12] Both kinds assume teachers learn throughout their lifetimes. Routine experts learn how to apply a core set of skills with greater fluency and efficiency. Adaptive experts, on the other hand, continually expand the breadth and depth of their expertise and are tuned into situations in which their skills are inadequate. Teachers with adaptive expertise, therefore, have the capability to identify when known routines do not work and to seek new information about different approaches when needed.[13]

In the next sections of this chapter, I provide an overview of the processes involved in developing adaptive expertise that moves through cycles of inquiry and knowledge-building and then discuss what it means for school, local authority and district leaders to promote and support this kind of learning for the teachers for whom they have responsibility.

Identifying students' knowledge and skills

The inquiry cycle begins and ends with students. Teaching is a highly contextualized activity in which competent teachers constantly adapt their practice as they respond to their students. These classroom experiences, together with the overall school environment developed by leaders, is an integral part of what teachers believe and how they think about their teaching.[14] They need to be considered in any professional learning activity. Professional development that focuses on new practices decontextualized from the immediate demands of students within a teacher's class is not likely to be translated into that environment. Teachers might find the information interesting but rarely apply it in their classrooms.

They are too busy with the competing and immediate demands of their students and the curriculum content that needs to be taught when they return to spend time trying to fit in something new that does not seem to be directly relevant.

Instead, professional learning should start with teachers asking themselves some direct and focused questions about what their students need to know and do, together with the more specific questions in the box below.

- What knowledge and skills do our students need to meet curricula, personal and social goals?
- What do they already know?
- What sources of evidence have we used and how adequate are they?
- What do they need to learn and do?
- How do we build on what they know?

Answering these questions requires focused assessment. Leaders and teachers need to know how to gather detailed diagnostic information about the knowledge and skills of individuals and groups of students to determine what is limiting their engagement and learning and might be contributing to their misunderstandings. The thrust of these investigations is usually defined in terms of a guiding curriculum or other goals of the system in which the school is located. The information on students gives leaders and teachers a clear picture of what these students know already and what is getting in the way of their learning. For many professionals in schools this is the first phase of their professional learning – how to undertake such assessments and how to interpret the information to identify teaching/learning challenges. For many teachers and even leaders, this shift involves taking a whole new perspective on the purposes of assessment as one of professional inquiry rather than one of grouping, labelling or credentialing students.

Determining what teachers need to know and be able to do

In the second part of the cycle, teachers identify what it is they need to know and do to be more effective, particularly with those students achieving less well than others. By teachers, I am referring to anyone with responsibility for student learning and well-being and may include teaching assistants for example. When teachers use evidence about their own students to determine what kind of professional learning they need, they are motivated by their own *need to know*. All too often professional development is motivated by someone else's *desire to tell*. In the latter situation, policy makers, researchers or professional development providers believe or have evidence that some kinds of teaching practice are more effective than others and create professional development opportunities to inform teachers about these practices without creating the need to know beyond compliance or teacher interest. They are then surprised that teachers are not very motivated to implement what is presented. As with most learners, the need to know provides a stronger motivation to engage than someone else's desire to tell.

> "Effective teacher professional learning is motivated by their need to know rather than someone else's desire to tell."

It is not easy for anyone to identify their own professional learning needs because it is difficult to step outside one's own frame of reference. Teachers often find that they need the assistance of others (facilitators, coaches or school leaders) to help them think about what makes the most sense for their learning. The questions below provide a framework for teachers to answer with a professional learning facilitator to establish their own learning needs.

- What knowledge and skills do we as professionals need to meet the learning needs of our students?
- How have we contributed to existing student outcomes?
- In what areas and with whom are we most effective?
- In what areas and with whom are we less effective and why?
- What do we already know that we can use to promote better outcomes?
- What do we need to learn and do to promote better outcomes?
- What sources of evidence/knowledge can we use?

To answer these questions, teachers need to link their findings from the first inquiry into students' profiles of learning and engagement to specific teaching practices. For many teachers, making these links is likely to involve looking at assessment information in new and challenging ways. The process can be uncomfortable for those involved because the spotlight starts to shift from what students know and can do to how well they have been taught. It can touch raw nerves, because asking themselves pointed questions like 'Has what I have done before been effective?' can impinge on teachers' sense of professional identity and competence. It is important to have a process for considering these possibilities and depersonalizing them to make it safe for teachers to inquire in this way about their practice.

Deepening professional knowledge

The next phase of the cycle is referred to as *deepening* professional knowledge and *refining* professional skills by engaging in further professional learning because the teachers involved already have considerable experience and are not starting as novices. Engaging in the first two dimensions of the cycle will have helped them identify what they need to learn but they usually also need to draw on the expertise of others to learn it. Teaching is a nuanced dance in which teachers integrate their knowledge of assessment, the curriculum, content knowledge and pedagogical content knowledge, in order to be responsive to students' needs. They move through a series of intricate steps to interpret the curriculum according to the specific learning needs of their students identified through assessment processes and adjust their practice accordingly.

Earlier, I emphasized the importance of new knowledge and skills introduced through professional learning situations being directly relevant to teachers' immediate classroom situation or they are likely to be forgotten. But it is only when this situational knowledge is understood in terms of the theory or principles underpinning it that teachers are able to retrieve and apply it appropriately in the moment-by-moment decisions they make every day in their classrooms. They need to be able to answer the question, 'Why is this particular approach more likely to be effective in this situation than another?' Otherwise, teaching becomes a process of trial and error. So an effective professional learning agenda includes a combination of theoretical knowledge and how it can be applied to solve specific problems of practice.

> **"It is only when situational knowledge is understood in terms of the theory or principles underpinning it that teachers are able to retrieve and apply it appropriately in the moment-by-moment decisions they make every day in their classrooms."**

Integration of the different kinds of knowledge together with their translation into practice means that teachers need multiple opportunities to learn over an extended time period. When new ideas are introduced they are usually only partially understood. Classroom try-outs bring up new issues. Ideas need to be revisited and clarified and tried out again. Over time, they deepen their understandings, retrieve knowledge more easily and enact their skills in the face of daily classroom challenges. It is quite possible to make superficial changes to practice within shorter time frames but the process does not achieve the kinds of deep learning that makes a sustainable difference to entrenched problems with student engagement, learning and well-being.

Engaging students in new learning experiences

Many studies have documented that teaching is the single most powerful system influence on student learning.[15] Little is likely to change for students if classroom teaching and learning activities do not change as a result of teachers' inquiry and knowledge development. As Richard Elmore explains, *changes within the instructional core are those that matter.*

Part of the process of professional learning, therefore, must be to apply new learning in practice and to view efforts to implement new ideas as part of learning. Professional learning cannot be seen as a process of acquiring then applying new knowledge. The knowledge and skills are acquired as much through the process of implementation as they are through someone describing or explaining theories and how to put them into practice. Thus, the analysis of classroom practice must be integral to the professional learning process. Knowledge is deepened through trying things out in practice.

> "Knowledge is deepened through trying things out in practice."

Assessing impact on student outcomes

The final question in the inquiry and knowledge-building cycles asks teachers and leaders to assess the impact of any changes on outcomes valued for the students. The contextualized nature of teaching practice – this teacher's skills with this group of students in this school environment – means there can be no guarantee that any specific teaching approach will have the anticipated result. The question for this part of the cycle and the sub-questions are in the box below.

- How effective has what we have learned and done been in promoting our students' learning?
- What should we keep going and what should we stop?
- What should we change or refine?
- What new challenges have become evident?

Assessing effectiveness is not a periodic event outside regular daily activities. It happens on a lesson-by-lesson, week-by-week and more long-term basis. The lesson-by-lesson check assesses students' immediate understandings of a particular lesson and what changes need to be made for the next lesson. Longer-term assessment ensures that the progress made is adequate against agreed benchmarks and identifies which areas need further work.

This checking process is an integral part of developing professional self-regulation – the key ingredient for deep learning. When teachers go back and check to see what difference their changes are making, they are also building their adaptive expertise through identifying what to keep as part of their regular routines, what needs to change and how they might access the expertise to develop more effective practice.[16]

Assessing impact is not the end of the cycle. As Figure 1.1 shows, the arrows keep cycling. If old problems persist, then it is time for different approaches to solving them. On the other hand, if desired changes are achieved in student outcomes, teachers who engage in the cycle as part of their professional routines usually identify new student challenges to work on as they delve deeper into the information about students and develop greater awareness of their own practice. In learning environments, the demands of teaching are never static.

Implications for the leadership of professional learning

Teachers are obviously key players in their learning but they can not do it alone. To achieve systemic change leaders need to support teachers to learn and change to meet the needs of their students. In a recent meta-analysis of the impact of school leadership on student outcomes, Robinson and colleagues found that the dimension with the strongest effect was leaders' promotion of and participation in the learning of their students.[17]

These findings raise the question: How can leaders support teacher learning when they cannot be experts in the full range of curriculum areas as well as knowing how to support students' engagement and well-being? At a minimum, leaders need to be sufficiently involved in the teachers' professional learning that they know what they should do to challenge and support their teachers. This minimum role involves ensuring that the conditions for teachers to learn and to implement the focus of that learning in their classrooms are established. However, creating a learning system within schools where all are committed to learning requires much more. It involves a shift in leadership mindsets in the same way as teachers must change their mindsets if they are to engage fully in professional learning.[18]

I recently studied how five particularly effective school leaders undertook this role. They were judged to be effective in terms of having very high increases in their students' literacy achievement and were seen to be instrumental in achieving these increases. These leaders thought of the teachers as 'their class' in the same way that teachers have a class of students. They saw it as their job, with the assistance of external experts, to promote the learning of 'their class' of professionals. In most situations leaders cannot know everything 'their class' of teachers needs to know, and will probably need to engage others with specific expertise. How these highly effective leaders approached their roles

> **"At a minimum, leaders need to be sufficiently involved in the teachers' professional learning that they know what they should do to challenge and support their teachers."**

and responsibilities was to work alongside the external experts to develop learning goals and plans with and for their teachers, as they expected their teachers to do with and for their students. Learning plans for teachers are just as important as learning plans for students if entrenched problems of teaching and learning are to be addressed.

Leaders also have new things to learn if they are to be effective in their role. In fact, they can also profit from systematically engaging in their own inquiry and knowledge-building cycles by identifying professional learning goals for themselves and seeking the appropriate expertise to achieve them, as illustrated in Figure 1.2. When leaders at the level of the school, local authority or district engage in these cycles of inquiry, they also become adaptive experts at the organizational level. They learn when existing routines work so they can be maintained, and also establish when they, as leaders, need to expand the depth and breadth of their current expertise because established routines are not as effective as they might be.

Taking such an approach across local authorities, districts and schools may seem overwhelming for some leaders. Like teachers, when faced with such a challenge, the temptation is to continue with previous practice. Let the teachers decide what they would

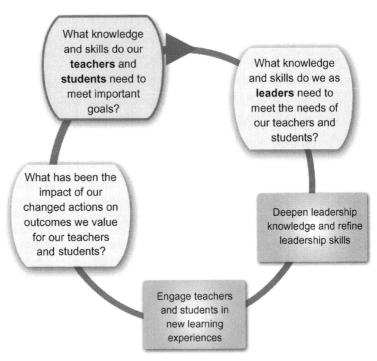

Figure 1.2 Leader inquiry and knowledge-building cycle to promote valued teaching and student outcomes

like to do. Just work with those prepared to volunteer. But, just like teachers, leaders cannot choose to work only with those willing to work with them and leave the others to do what they like in the classroom if the difference is to be made for *all* students. There is also considerable evidence from the best evidence synthesis on professional learning and development that involving volunteers had no greater impact than requiring teachers to participate. More important than volunteering is that the teachers become engaged in the professional learning at some point together with its implications for teaching practice. Leaders, therefore, need to meet the challenge of ensuring all teachers are engaged. Otherwise their schools will consist of patches of brilliance for the engaged and mediocrity or worse for those who are not.

Achieving a systemic lift in student engagement and learning to meet the challenges of change means that all educators throughout the system need to learn how to enact their roles and responsibilities in ways that focus on and achieve those outcomes valued for students. Teachers cannot be expected to solve the difficult problems of student engagement, learning and well-being on their own. They need learning leaders who can provide the right support for teachers to learn, so that they, in turn, promote their students' learning. They need to work in a system that learns. A system lift requires a systemic response.

Reflecting on your professional learning experiences

Think about the last time you either led or participated in some kind of professional learning. Together with those with whom you worked, decide if your activities were at a basic, developing or integrated level using the descriptors below. What evidence do you have to support your decision? Do others have evidence that leads to a different decision?

The reason to engage

Basic	Developing	Integrated
To find out about a new way to teach associated with improving practice and student outcomes	To solve a problem with student engagement, learning or well-being (e.g. improve reading comprehension)	To solve a specific problem with student engagement, learning or well-being as a result of close analysis of the information about students (e.g. limited vocabulary is affecting students' reading comprehension)

The knowledge and skills of focus

Basic	Developing	Integrated
Practical ideas about new strategies/ programmes were the focus	Specific, in-depth areas of assessment, curriculum or how to teach it but not integrated and generically linked to the problem trying to solve	Integration of in-depth knowledge about assessment, curriculum and how to teach it, specifically linked to problem trying to solve

The leaders' role

Basic	Developing	Integrated
Leaders selected the focus of professional learning for teachers, organized it then left the teachers to it OR teachers selected the focus without leaders	Leaders worked with teachers to identify the professional learning focus. Leaders were present during professional learning sessions and supported teachers when needed	Teachers and leaders worked together on: <ul><li>specific concerns about student engagement, learning or well-being;</li><li>knowledge and skills teachers needed to meet these concerns;</li><li>knowledge and skills leaders needed to help teachers to meet these concerns and who could help</li></ul>

If any of the activities were at a basic or developing level, decide together what each of you needs to do to move them towards becoming more integrated. What evidence might you collect to monitor if your activities are moving closer to the description at the integrated level? Decide when you will check your progress and how you will do it.

2

Finding Out About Students

The inquiry and knowledge-building cycle begins with an analysis of students' needs. Focusing on students reinforces for teachers that the primary purpose for participating in professional learning is to enhance those student outcomes that are valued by the community

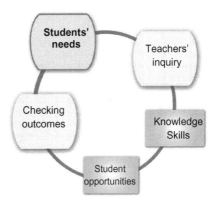

within which the students live and learn – learning outcomes, engagement outcomes and well-being outcomes. Outcomes for students become the reason for teachers to engage in professional learning.

For this focus to have meaning and impact, however, it is important to attend to a mix of purposes, processes and relationships. In this chapter I consider this mix in relation to using assessment information for professional learning, collecting and analysing high-quality evidence and having conversations about the interpretation of that evidence.

Using assessment information for professional learning

The primary purpose for analysing students' needs in professional learning situations is to shape ongoing professional learning and teaching practice. If this is not the purpose, teachers are likely to default to the position that gathering information about students is about students alone and not about teaching or themselves as professionals. This is particularly so when teachers have traditionally assessed students for the purposes of awarding grades, reporting these grades to others, or grouping students in class. Traditional grading and reporting is often underpinned by a belief in a fixed notion of student ability – students learn what they are capable of learning and there is little that teachers can do about it. Under these circumstances teachers may question what they can learn from unpacking information about students apart from being more accurate in their grading or reporting practices. Before teachers can use information about students in much depth for their teaching, they need to understand the underlying reasons for assessing students and have opportunities to explore the conflicts inherent in the different purposes.

> **"If improving outcomes for students is not the purpose of professional learning, teachers are likely to default to the position that collecting information about students is not about teaching."**

Because it is so fundamental to the success of creating meaningful change in classroom teaching and learning, I will return to this theme of engaging teachers' beliefs and the potential for conflict between existing beliefs and those underpinning professional learning processes throughout this book. As an eminent group of scholars in the United States[19] have told us, when teachers' prior knowledge and beliefs are not engaged and the implications for practice clearly understood, teachers usually adopt new ideas at a superficial level only, while believing they understand them more deeply. This happens because they interpret new ideas in terms of their existing cognitive frameworks and believe their existing practice is more similar to the new ideas than it really is. When this happens they are likely to just tweak what they already do rather than changing it more fundamentally as intended by those promoting change. These authors refer to the problem as one of 'over-assimilation'. Sometimes this kind of superficial tweaking is seen as teachers resisting new ideas, but in reality the ideas have never been understood in any depth. So, if the purpose for collecting assessment information on students is to provide a focus for professional learning, it is critical to engage teachers' existing ideas about assessment – its purposes and its use.

In their landmark book *How People Learn*, John Bransford and colleagues from the National Research Council in the United States[20] also identified the importance of engaging prior understandings if any learner is to understand the difference between the beliefs they hold and the beliefs underpinning new ideas. In a summary booklet for practitioners, these researchers expressed their findings in terms of students, but acknowledged they apply equally to teachers, so I have adapted their wording to be more directly applicable to professional learning:

Teachers come to the classroom with preconceptions about how the world works, including how students learn and how best to teach them. In professional learning situations, if initial understandings are not engaged, they may fail to grasp new concepts and information that are presented or may participate for the purposes of compliance but revert to their preconceptions once back in the classroom.[21]

Another important element to consider when assessment information is used for professional learning is to ensure that what is assessed relates to the outcomes that matter. Curriculum documents or other goals are likely to form the basis of the outcomes that are assessed. In many countries a recent emphasis has been to focus on literacy and numeracy because of their fundamental role in achievement in other curriculum areas and in creating life opportunities. More sophisticated assessments have been developed in these areas than in others. Some educators believe that this emphasis has been at the cost of a wider and richer curriculum. If there is no shared understanding of what matters, it is easy to fall into the trap of valuing what is readily assessed, rather than working out how to assess what is valued.

Having and using high-quality evidence

If evidence about students' engagement, learning and well-being is to be used as the basis for professional learning, then it is important that the evidence is of sufficiently high quality for teachers to have the information they need. Otherwise teachers' valuable time can be wasted. In this next section I highlight two important attributes: that the assessment information is fit for the purpose of promoting teacher learning and that the procedures used attend to issues of validity and reliability.

Fit-for-purpose assessments

The assessment instruments and processes selected must provide the information required to inform what needs to happen for students to reach the outcomes desired. At its most basic, this means using fit-for-purpose assessment tools. At this stage of the cycle these tools need to provide sufficiently detailed information to give direction to professional learning endeavours. For example, if the goal is to improve student engagement, then an assessment instrument or process that provides profiles of situations associated with high and low engagement for different groups of students is more useful than a generic engagement index. If the goal is for reading comprehension to be at a state, provincial or national level, then the use of an assessment tool that provides norm-referenced information is essential to demonstrate whether or not student progress is adequate. However, norm-referenced assessments are not necessarily sufficient as a basis for establishing professional learning foci, unless they provide rich diagnostic information as well as normative information. Finding out that a student is reading more than two years behind their peers provides a platform for further investigation, not one for deciding on specific directions for professional learning. Many norm-referenced assessments do provide diagnostic information but their potential for doing this often goes untapped because teachers and parents focus on the aggregate score or level rather than analysing the tasks in which students did well and those that were not done so well. It is well established that when students are given a mark for their work, they tend to ignore the comments designed to help them do better.[22] The same can happen with the adults teaching the students. The awarding of scores or level designations for students can lead to

> **"Fit-for-purpose assessments provide sufficiently detailed information to give direction to professional learning."**

a focus on the score rather than analysing students' work to find out what teachers need to teach better.

Sometimes teachers use a battery of assessments at the beginning or end of the year with no specific purpose in mind, apart from identifying where students are at. This practice is unlikely to meet the requirements for using fit-for-purpose assessments. Having large quantities of information is not the same as having high-quality information. Quality tends to improve as teachers and their leaders engage in iterative cycles of inquiry to build their pedagogical content knowledge, identify better questions to ask and seek more detailed evidence to answer them. As they become more sophisticated in analysing student needs, the evidence sought becomes a search for answers to specific questions about specific puzzles evident in students' learning profiles. Teachers are likely to draw on a mix of norm-referenced assessments, teacher designed assessment tasks, and more informal processes such as observing students and analysing students' work. The case below shows the development through iterative inquiry cycles of a group of teachers in one school. Like other cases throughout this book, it begins with a quote from one of the participants.

'The data didn't tell us what we needed to know.'[23]

(School leader)

In this school with high numbers of English language learners, students were assessed each year on a generic reading test that provided a single score that showed them to be, on average, well below their peers. The teachers identified that they needed to focus on reading and how to teach it more effectively, but after working with a reading specialist realized they needed to know much more before they could address the problem. With specialist guidance they analysed the kinds of errors the students had made on the reading test and identified that word recognition scores were similar to other students of the same age, but paragraph comprehension was poor. Scores improved after the teachers learned new teaching strategies for improving paragraph comprehension and involved the community in relevant out-of-school activities. The improvements, however, did not match the vision of these students working at levels similar to national profiles of achievement.

On the next iteration of the inquiry cycle the teachers demanded the use of an assessment instrument that gave them more sophisticated diagnostic information. As a result, they found that although many of these students could recognize words, understanding their meaning was not sufficient to provide a basis for good comprehension. Once again drawing the community in and working in class with an emphasis on vocabulary development led to further improvement, but the students' reading comprehension still did not reach the desired levels. The teachers had a hunch that the students' knowledge of technical vocabulary was tripping them up so they decided to investigate this possibility. Working through another iteration of the cycle led to more detailed understanding that these second language learners were able to read and interpret the technical language (so the teachers' hunch was wrong) but had problems with the kinds of metaphorical and colloquial vocabulary used in the texts. With further teacher learning and new opportunities for students to learn, the students' profiles of achievement were finally indistinguishable from those nationally.

It is often difficult to identify fit-for-purpose assessments for student outcomes falling outside literacy and numeracy. There are assessment instruments available but their more limited range presents a challenge to ensure that what is assessed provides adequate information. Teachers need to find a range of sources to gather sufficient evidence to make decisions. They might use observations of students as they learn and interact, specially designed assessment tasks, analysis of students' work, as well as interviews to ascertain understandings and viewpoints.

Procedures that provide valid and reliable information

Because the information that is generated about students will form the basis for decisions about professional learning, in the service of student learning, it is important that teachers have confidence in the quality of evidence they are considering. These are issues of reliability, that is, the judgements made are accurate and can be trusted; and validity, that is, they are reasonable and relate to the important dimensions being considered. As is always the case, reliability and validity issues differ according to the evidence collected. If comparisons with some kind of benchmarks, such as national, state or provincial standards are to be made, then the procedures for collecting the assessment information must be consistent with the administration and scoring protocols of these assessments, otherwise the comparison is invalid. In those situations where scoring relies on teacher interpretation, it is important that moderation procedures are put in place to ensure one teacher gives the same score to a piece of work as another and that these scores are consistent with the criteria intended on the assessment. Just reaching agreement between the teachers is not sufficient because the teachers might all be wrong. The important issue is to understand the scoring criteria in sufficient depth to be able to critique one another's judgements according to the criteria. In many situations, developing these kinds of understandings forms a powerful professional learning opportunity because the critique often deepens knowledge.

On the other hand, if a deeper diagnosis of students' learning strategies is the objective, then how the information is collected will need to be more flexible and focus on creating and capturing opportunities in teaching and learning situations.

Considerations around analysis follow similar lines. Analysis of non-standardized diagnostic information needs to focus on the light it sheds on the problem being investigated. Norm-referenced assessments typically have standard procedures for analysis. These analyses can provide information about the adequacy of students' levels of achievement and the progress they have made since the last time they were formally assessed. These two pieces of information go hand in hand and both are important. Whether or not particular rates of progress are of concern, for example, depends on where students are in relation to their colleagues. Students well behind others need to make accelerated progress to catch up. Students well

> **"Data collection and analysis need to provide information on levels and rates of progress plus diagnostic information."**

ahead of others should continue to aim for faster than expected progress and should not be held back. Data collection and analysis need to provide information on levels and rates of progress plus diagnostic information.

When examining levels and rates of progress, it is important to disaggregate the information to ensure all students are considered, including particular subgroups of concern. Averages hide variability. Schools sometimes have above-average achievement overall that hides the groups of students bumping along the bottom of the distribution. When progress is being considered, it is possible for a school to improve student achievement on average over a number of years, but actually have a decline in the progress of some groups because improvements for the majority hides the minority.

Levels of analysis and aggregation are also important for professional learning purposes. Analyses that include all students in a grade or year level do not identify whether one class of students is learning faster and more deeply than another. Teachers need to know how all their students are progressing by asking themselves, 'Am I more effective with the lower achieving students and could I be holding back the high fliers?' 'Is it the English language learners who are falling behind so I need to know more about the specific learning needs of these students and how to teach them?' While disaggregating assessment information by class may not be acceptable for accountability purposes because of other factors that come into play in determining achievement, this kind of disaggregation is important for teachers to identify their specific professional learning needs.

Collecting information over time can also add to the richness of the diagnosis of students' learning needs. For some socio-economic groups, the combined impact of end-of-year wind-up activities in schools, school holidays and a delayed start to beginning-of-year teaching (known collectively as the 'summer effect') can lead to significant drops in student achievement.[24] It is only through assessing students at the beginning and end of the year over a number of years that this kind of pattern becomes apparent. When the summer effect shows greater drops than the effect over the school year in terms of expected progress, students can actually go backwards in relation to their peers. In these situations, the professional learning focus needs to be very different from those situations in which the summer effect is less but students make less progress over the school year. How the teachers in one school investigated the summer effect is described in the following case.

'We thought we were making progress but we were actually going backwards.'[25]

(School leader)

A school serving a low socio-economic community had engaged in an intensive school reform process with a focus on literacy for two years. They worked with a professional learning facilitator and were pleased with the improvement in reading and writing scores between the beginning and end of the year. Students were making far greater gains than expected according to the test norms. When they began the third year by analysing the student assessment information to determine their professional learning goals, they were puzzled about why their beginning of year scores for each grade level were so similar to the beginning of the previous year. For two grade levels, they were actually lower. If the students were making such good progress during the year, why did they start so low at the beginning of the next year? Through discussing the data patterns with the professional learning facilitator, they came up with the 'summer effect' as a possible explanation. Sure enough, a longitudinal analysis of the data showed a large drop between the assessment at the end of each year and the beginning of the next.

Their initial reaction was to think about how they could intervene with families to ensure reading continued over the holiday period. However, one teacher counted the number of weeks students were in school and on holiday between the two assessments. She reported that the students actually had more time in school over this time than they had on holiday. The teachers realized that they could be contributing to the summer effect in two ways. Essentially they stopped their formal literacy programmes several weeks before the end of the year and took several weeks to pick them up at the beginning of the new year. After further discussion, they also realized that their literacy programmes did not orient the students to taking responsibility for maintaining their reading over the holiday break. They had unwittingly created student dependency on them to engage in literacy learning. The challenge was to create greater student autonomy.

As a result, they developed a three-pronged approach to address the summer effect. One was to work with the parents and community. Another was to be more deliberate about their beginning and end-of-year literacy programmes. The third was to show the patterns of assessment information to the students and get them to help the teachers to work out how the students could take more responsibility for engaging in relevant literacy activities.

It is all about interpretation

In practice, deciding what outcomes are valued, deciding what assessment information to collect and how to analyse it all come together to form a rich mix. Interpretation is about shaping the information, organizing it, and thinking about what it might mean through iterative cycles rather than through sequential steps. When teachers engage in processes of making meaning, they often come to an awareness of the need to go deeper – to undertake different kinds of analyses or collect additional information because important questions cannot be answered from the information available.

Through all these iterations, however, it is important to distinguish between the raw assessment data together with basic analyses of means and variability, and the interpretations of that data. Data do not speak for themselves. People make sense of data through an interpretive process and turn data or evidence into information and insights. As the case above on the summer effect shows, it is this meaning-making process that counts. It would have been easy for the teachers to blame the parents for the summer effect without examining their own role in creating it. Instead they checked their individual and collective interpretations and came to much richer understandings and solutions.

What the case of the summer effect also shows is that making meaning from assessment information requires new kinds of conversations. All too often data are presented to teachers, possibly with a leader providing his or her interpretation, as if this interpretation was the only valid one. Teachers then look at the data and privately accept or reject the leaders' interpretation. In essence they make sense of it privately (or possibly with a small group of colleagues), then go about the business of teaching with the data having little influence on what happens.

The problem underlying this scenario is that the interpretations we make depend on our personal theories about what leads to what. A theory is just a set of linked ideas, so a personal theory about student assessment information comprises linking beliefs about what the data show, what has led to the data looking like they do, and what should be done about it. Simple theories explaining the summer effect is that parents do not value reading so do not bother to read to their children or provide them with books over the summer holidays. Their personal theories about what is important may have closed them to alternative possibilities.

A more sophisticated theory is that parents do value reading but do not know how to go about encouraging their children to engage in specific literacy practices over the summer. Even more sophisticated is including one's own actions in the theory. In the case above, the teachers were open to considering their place in the theory and realized that they may have adopted literacy teaching approaches throughout the year that created dependency so students had not developed the knowledge and skills to take responsibility for their own learning. This theory has implications for professional learning.

Personal theories not only influence the process of interpretation, they also shape what assessment information is collected in the first place. In the case of English language learners with low comprehension, the teachers held personal theories about the difficulties these students might be having with technical vocabulary. They decided to collect data to test these theories. Fortunately, they were also open to alternative interpretations and noticed quite different patterns in the data.

> **"Personal theories not only influence the process of interpretation, they also shape what assessment information is collected in the first place."**

This case also illustrates that the process of assessment and the process of teaching are not separate but rather form integrated activities. Using assessment information for teaching and learning is not an extended process of testing, analysis, interpretation, followed by teaching. Rather it is a process of being constantly on the lookout for new information to confirm or disconfirm personal theories through everyday teaching and learning activities. At times, these activities need to be interrupted for the collection of more formal assessment information.

The process of developing personal theories from simple versions based on untested assumptions to more nuanced versions that challenge and expand assumptions depends in large part on having conversations with others who can contribute alternative viewpoints and have deep knowledge of effective teaching and learning processes. The kinds of conversations described in the cases above help to make assumptions explicit and available for exploration, so that the participants can learn faster and more deeply. Lorna Earl

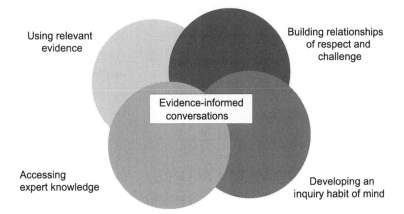

Figure 2.1 Evidence-informed conversations
Source: Adapted from Earl, L. and Timperley, H. (2008) *Professional Learning Conversation: Challenges in Using Evidence for Improvement.* London: Springer Academic Publishers.

and I[26] developed a model for thinking about these conversations that I have modified and presented in Figure 2.1.

The model proposes four important components in evidence-informed conversations. The first, using relevant evidence, has been the main focus of this chapter already so I will not elaborate it further. The second involves developing an inquiry habit of mind, which in essence is the habit of needing to know and valuing deep learning. Engaging in the inquiry and knowledge-building cycle both develops and becomes dependent on having an inquiry habit of mind. Teachers do not necessarily come to the professional learning situation with this orientation and do not need to be predisposed to having an inquiry orientation to their work before engaging in the cycle. Rather, facilitated engagement in the process itself creates the inquiry habit of mind. At some point, however, the teachers need to have such an orientation if they are to take control of the process for themselves.

The third component of Figure 2.1 involves building relationships of respect and challenge. Teachers cannot readily engage in cycles of inquiry and knowledge-building when they feel criticized or put down for not being good enough. However, challenge also forms part of the equation because it is hard to learn if interactions always affirm and support what teachers are doing rather than challenging them to improve teaching and learning. Thus this component includes both challenge and support.

Developing inquiry habits of mind and building relationships of respect and challenge complement one another because they are mutually interdependent. Inquiry habits of mind are fostered within relationships of respect and challenge. Each involves the need to know, questioning assumptions and focusing on what makes a difference. I have drawn parallels between developing inquiry habits of mind and building relationships of respect and challenge for each of these components in Table 2.1.

I will describe briefly what is meant by the three qualities listed in Table 2.1. The need to know means that the motivation for collecting and interpreting assessment information comes from trying to solve teaching and learning problems. Because deep understanding is valued, teachers are open to a variety of interpretations about what the assessment information might mean for their own practice. It also means that tentativeness is brought to its use and interpretation because education is full of uncertainties. It does not mean using evidence about students and teaching to prove a particular point or to fight turf wars.

Questioning assumptions requires that the assumptions underpinning personal theories are made explicit, the conversations help to unpack the implications of these assumptions for teaching and learning, evidence that supports or contradicts them is considered,

REALIZING THE POWER OF PROFESSIONAL LEARNING

Table 2.1 Parallel components of inquiry habits of mind and relationships
of respect and challenge

Developing inquiry habits of mind	Building relationships of respect and challenge
The need to know Teachers create the need to know and value deep understandings about their own and others' practice for the purpose of improvement	Relationships are based on assumptions about the capacity for all to learn as an ongoing process of needing to know. They respect that the need to know is full of pitfalls and mistakes – reaching deep understandings needs deep discussion
Questioning assumptions Teachers are open to questioning the assumptions that make up their personal theories as well as seeking support for them because questioning improves the quality of interpretation of information	Relationships involve challenging each other's assumptions that underpin personal theories in ways that give teachers confidence they will not be ridiculed or put down
Focusing on what makes a difference Teachers focus on what they and the school have influence over and can do something about	Those involved do not play blame games about others but similarly do not accept responsibility for those areas they cannot influence

and diversity of views is valued because diversity helps to challenge what is sometimes taken for granted. It does not mean treating statements as self-evident or accepting a particular point of view as valid just because someone believes it to be so.

Focusing on what makes a difference brings a non-blame orientation to teaching and learning. Children attend school to be educated and teaching has the greatest systems' influence on outcomes[27] so what happens in schools and classrooms is of paramount importance. However, teachers cannot be held responsible for all the ills of society or expect to make much progress in extreme circumstances without additional support and sometimes specific interventions. On the other hand, there are many examples of situations where schools located in communities under stress have made extraordinary progress with effective leadership and teaching. The question these schools ask is, 'How can we mitigate these community circumstances within the school environment?' rather than 'How can we expect much from students who come from these communities?'

The final circle in Figure 2.1 is one I have added to the original. It refers to accessing expert knowledge. Inquiry without reference to what is already known to be effective raises the very real possibility of reinventing wheels and wasting valuable teacher and student learning time. At worst it results in bringing ineffective strategies to solve urgent problems. Over the last 15 years knowledge about effective practices, particularly to accelerate the progress of lower achieving students, has grown appreciably and is available on websites, in books and papers and through engagement with experts in given areas. Assuming that knowledge for teaching must be locally developed is to ignore one of the basic tenets of being professional; that practice is based on a body of systematically developed, scientific knowledge and that this knowledge is applied in the interests and service of their clients.[28] Much of the material in this book is about accessing this kind of knowledge for professional learning so I will leave further discussion of this fourth circle to later chapters in this book.

43

Reflecting on your professional learning experiences

Think about the last time you engaged in some kind of analysis of student assessment information. Together with those with whom you worked, decide if your activities were at a basic, developing or integrated level using the descriptors below. What evidence do you have to support your decision? Do others have evidence that leads to a different decision?

Using student assessment information to understand professional learning implications

Basic	Developing	Integrated
Student assessment information is seen to reflect student abilities rather than linked to teaching implications	Student assessment information is studied for implications for teaching and it is assumed that teachers are able to act on the information to address identified student learning needs	Student assessment information is closely analysed for specific implications for teaching and for professional learning

Use of fit-for-purpose assessments

Basic	Developing	Integrated
Students routinely assessed using a single assessment that is assumed to be assessing the outcomes valued and to be appropriate for all contexts	Students routinely assessed using a range of assessment instruments and processes but their diagnostic qualities are not explicitly linked to specific questions or agreed outcomes	Students assessed to answer specific questions about teaching and learning issues in relation to outcomes agreed to by the community in which the students live and learn

Conversations for interpretation

Basic	Developing	Integrated
Conversations comprise one person presenting assessment information to teachers, providing an interpretation, and leaving teachers to make meaning of the implications for teaching and learning	Conversations involve most teachers actively interpreting the implications of the data for teaching and learning but the personal theories underpinning different interpretations are not discussed	Conversations actively challenge teachers' personal theories about reasons for patterns in the assessment information and the teaching implications made from it. Ways of testing disagreements are developed

If any of the activities were at a basic or developing level, decide together what each of you needs to do to move them towards becoming more integrated. What evidence might you collect to monitor if your activities are moving closer to the description at the integrated level? Decide when you will check your progress and how you will do it.

3

Building Teacher Knowledge

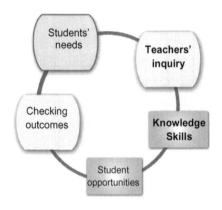

This chapter is about teacher learning – what is it that teachers need to learn and do to make a difference to their students? It describes the next two dimensions of the inquiry and knowledge-building cycle presented in Chapter 1. The first of these dimensions is the identification of the knowledge and skills teachers need to learn based on the knowledge and skills students need to learn (Chapter 2). The second is actually engaging in professional learning to deepen knowledge and refine skills. These two dimensions are identified separately in the cycle because, all too often, professional learning begins with a district or school leader, or the teachers themselves, deciding what teachers need to learn and then arranging some kind of professional development opportunities for them to learn it. Then they wonder why the professional learning does not lead to substantive changes to practice and improvement in outcomes for students. When the professional learning is not driven by identified student and teacher needs, teachers might find the experience interesting but in the absence of a need to solve a specific problem of practice or to improve a particular outcome for students, there is little urgency or motivation to change and improve. Substantive change that will have an impact on entrenched problems of student engagement, learning or well-being takes far more effort than continuing with current routines and practice or maybe tweaking them a little. It requires high levels of motivation and a willingness to stay the course.

The evidence-informed conversations identified in Chapter 2 were related to students, but the same processes apply to unpacking what teachers need to learn and do to create better outcomes for students. At no point in the cycle is it more important to ensure that the accumulated evidence is relevant, the people involved approach the process with inquiry habits of mind, there is access to expert knowledge and there are relationships of trust and challenge. These are the components identified in Figure 2.1 in the previous chapter. Part of developing respect and challenge is that teachers trust their colleagues and have confidence that they will be supported to make the necessary changes and improvements to

> "When the professional learning is not driven by identified student and teacher needs, teachers might find the experience interesting but in the absence of a need to solve a specific problem of practice or to improve a particular outcome for students, there is little urgency or motivation to change and improve."

achieve a realistic vision of some alternative. Unrealistic visions and critique without support can be destructive of both teacher motivation and confidence.

Identifying teachers' learning needs

Increasingly, teachers are expected to shape their teaching in ways that are responsive to the diverse learning needs of their students. It is not surprising that formative assessment processes have been demonstrated to improve student motivation, engagement and learning, because they are based on both students' and teachers' understanding of where students are at in relation to a goal, and what they need to do next to reach it.[29] In the same way, teachers' motivation, engagement and learning increases when they are supported to identify where they are at in relation to a goal and what they need to do next to reach it. Teachers can be as diverse as their students in what they believe to be effective and how they approach their teaching tasks. This diversity is often not catered for in professional learning situations. Richard Elmore[30] claims that one of the strongest social norms in schools is that everyone is expected to pretend they are equally effective in what they do, even when they feel unprepared to do it. Having to pretend is the antithesis of learning.

Making teacher learning needs explicit is counter-cultural to the norm of silence about the effectiveness of teaching practices. Traditional forms of professional development are not necessarily seen by teachers as learning opportunities to improve practice or student outcomes. Suzanne Wilson and Jennifer Berne[31] identified that teachers come to many professional development sessions believing they have little to learn and have few expectations to change their practice as a result of their participation. On the other hand, those who lead such sessions usually believe that teachers have much to learn and change. Unless these differences are discussed, and the reason for providing the learning opportunities is made explicit, it is likely that both groups will remain frustrated by the other's undisclosed beliefs.

> "Teachers come to many professional development sessions believing they have little to learn and have few expectations to change their practice as a result of their participation."

One way of addressing this problem is for teachers to develop learning goals. Formative assessment research tells us that students are more motivated when they have challenging learning goals. In the same way teachers are more likely to be motivated to engage with professional learning if it addresses challenging learning goals for themselves. If those goals are to have an impact on students' engagement, learning and well-being, however, then they must address both their students' needs and their own. It is important that they begin this dimension of the inquiry and knowledge-building cycle, therefore, by working together with someone with appropriate expertise to answer the main question in Figure 1.1 and the more detailed sub-questions that follow.

- What knowledge and skills do we as professionals need to meet the needs of our students (learning goals)?
- How have we contributed to existing student outcomes?
- In what areas and with whom are we effective?
- In what areas and with whom are we less effective and why?

- What do we already know that we can use to promote valued outcomes?

- What do we need to learn and do to promote these outcomes and what are our learning goals?

- What sources of evidence/knowledge can we use?

The depth to which teachers answer these questions usually evolves through iterations of the inquiry and knowledge-building cycle. As teachers become familiar with the process and its purpose, analysing student data, analysing teaching practice, and establishing learning goals become routine.

To answer the first sub-question about how they may have contributed to existing student outcomes, teachers and leaders need to work together moving between outcomes for students and teaching approaches as they consider both what has worked well and areas of need. This investigation should build teachers' sense of self-efficacy as they identify what they do well and give them confidence that they will be supported to become more effective in the areas they do not do so well. This process is particularly important when teachers are working in situations where they have come to hold low expectations of students. Low expectations usually arise when teachers have tried repeatedly to change student behaviour or learning, with limited success. It is reasonable under these circumstances for teachers to expect little from, or for, students and sometimes even to blame them. Low expectations can quickly become endemic throughout a school as teachers and leaders feel powerless to change what is happening. For low expectations to change, new ways of thinking and practice need to be introduced systematically through processes that help teachers achieve better outcomes so they come to believe they can make more of a difference for their students. They can start this process by identifying what they do well and how the students responded. Addressing low expectations takes time, persistence and a great deal of support. Here is how one secondary school approached a problem with high student suspensions that teachers blamed on the students.

'It is all the students' fault.'[32]

(Secondary schoolteacher)

This large multicultural secondary school had high rates of student suspension from school. The teachers routinely sent misbehaving students out of class to senior staff members who removed them from the school for varying lengths of time depending on the frequency and severity of the offences. Their approach was based on a philosophy that teachers cannot be expected to deal with these difficult students who should be held responsible for their actions and by suspending them they would realize they needed to behave in class. The local education office challenged the school about the high suspension rates and pointed out that suspending students was inconsistent with the school's goal of having a safe social and emotional environment. This goal was being selectively applied and jeopardizing the safety of those students who were being suspended. A senior staff member responsible for student guidance took the opportunity to lead a team of teachers in an analysis of the problem and a consideration of literature related to student misbehaviour. They found that the high suspension rates were actually connected to a small number of students with repeated suspensions. They also became aware of differences among the staff. While some believed that students should be held solely responsible for their behaviour and face the consequences, others felt that behaviour was a function of relationships, connectedness and respect among students and between teachers and students.

The staff spent a series of staff meetings engaging in this analysis of the problem and the outcomes of their current response to student misbehaviour with an expert in restorative justice that focuses on the relationships and connectedness between teachers and students with the management of student behaviour being seen as a joint responsibility. The teachers identified that their relationships with most students was positive. Many students, for example, were engaged in extra-curricular programmes provided by the teachers. When they considered which students were being suspended, they agreed that their relationships with these disengaged students were not very good and it was easier to get rid of them than to try to engage with them. They accepted the possibility (with reservations initially) that if they learned how to interact with these students differently, outcomes might be different.

Understanding what the principles of restorative justice really meant in terms of both philosophy and practice took some time. Initially the practices were superficially adopted as a behaviour management strategy because this was the student problem they were trying to solve. Over time their understanding of the philosophy deepened and so did changes to their practice through engagement in dedicated staff meetings and restorative conversations guided by staff from each department trained specifically to provide this support.

The actions of one teacher provide an example of how the new knowledge and experiences affected her practice. She had attended the staff meeting and agreed to try the restorative justice approach. When she faced a disruptive student in class, she tried to be less confrontational in ways they had talked about. It did not work so she sent the student out of the room to the senior staff member as she had in the past. She was surprised (and not pleased) when the senior staff member told her that she was expected to have a restorative conversation with the student supported by the senior staff member. She was not accustomed to having her practice questioned and had not realized that getting the student's perspective on the way she had dealt with his behaviour was to be part of the process. However, through listening to the student about what was going wrong for him in class and having the opportunity to express what was happening for her at both a personal and professional level led to new understandings and a different relationship. Over time and a number of such incidents she came to understand what was involved and became a strong advocate.

Over a period of two years, suspensions declined from a high of 3.5 per cent of students per year to just 1.0 per cent and the teachers talked about the 'more collaborative and relaxed atmosphere with expectations of connection and relating'.

This case illustrates several key ideas related to using learning conversations to identify teacher learning (see the description from Earl and Timperley in Chapter 2). Having relevant data was essential when these teachers investigated the links between their teaching practices and outcomes for students. The comparative suspension rates and records of teachers' referral practices were pivotal to move this conversation from one of blaming the students to examining how practice needed to change. Relationships were also important. Having respectful but challenging conversations permeated the interactions. Teachers were not berated for sending students out of class, nor were continued dismissals accepted without an analysis of what had happened from both the student's and the teacher's perspective. Inquiry habits of mind developed over a period of implementation. Teachers did not come to the initial staff meeting seeking answers; rather, the openness to inquiry into the impact of their own actions developed as they participated in the requirement to do something different for disruptive students and came to realize there might be better ways to do things. Access to expert knowledge about how they could do things differently was essential to success. Imagine what would have happened if teachers had simply been told not to remove students from class anymore or that the school was going to suspend fewer students so they needed to deal with them, without the alternatives and the new learning that came from the expert in restorative justice and support from senior staff.

When teachers ask and answer the question about how they, as teachers, may be contributing to existing outcomes, it raises other questions of what teachers already know that they can use to promote valued outcomes and what they need to learn. Finding ways to identify learning needs for teachers is something that recurs as an issue among promoters and providers of professional learning. The next case illustrates similar processes to the case on restorative justice but with a more academic orientation.

> **"When teachers ask and answer the question about how they, as teachers, may be contributing to existing outcomes, it raises other questions of what teachers already know that they can use to promote valued outcomes and what they need to learn."**

'Now we know why they didn't get it.'[33]

(Teacher)

In this small primary school in a country town students' writing achievement was low. They had various experts come to talk to them but not much had changed. They decided to participate in the Literacy Professional Development Project (see Chapter 1) because they knew the outcomes were good and realized they needed to have deeper engagement with the problem. Initial observations by the visiting facilitator showed that their writing lessons were focused on motivating students to express something from within themselves, rather than on the skills and knowledge of how texts work and how to write for different communicative purposes. When the facilitator talked to some students during the observation about their understanding of the lesson, most did not know the lesson aims, the specific features of the writing purpose, or who they were writing for. They were also not sure how they could improve their writing or how their teacher could help them. The facilitator shared these responses with the teachers.

At the following staff meeting, the facilitator summarized the teaching practices she observed and invited the teachers to add anything she had missed. She then asked them why they had chosen these particular practices explaining it would help her to understand why they approached the teaching of writing in the way they did. The teachers explained their beliefs in terms of the need to motivate students to write because so many were reluctant writers. She then asked them to identify the consequences of this approach, which included concerns about achievement, limited student understanding of purpose, the learning aims, or how to improve.

The facilitator then suggested an alternative way of thinking about writing; that writing was for communication, with specific features associated with particular purposes, and that students needed to be clear about these purposes in order to improve. The teachers agreed that this was an area where they wanted to learn more.

Having established a focus for their own learning, the teachers actively sought the facilitator's assistance with professional readings, developing criteria for their observations of each other and how they could find out if their students understood their lesson aims. Over a number of visits from the facilitator to support the change, the teachers initially focused their writing programmes on recounts. They reported how they and their students had become much more engaged in writing lessons.

Four months later when the students were reassessed, their writing achievement for recounts had improved three times the expected annual rate nationally. Buoyed by their success, they then investigated the features of writing an argument, a very different purpose for writing.

The Earl and Timperley model for evidence-informed conversations also applies in this case. The students' levels of achievement and the observations of teaching practices were the relevant evidence that provided insight into the problem. It is often tempting to ask teachers about their own learning needs rather than to have them established through the use of evidence. However, when teachers in this project were asked to rate their confidence in different aspects of writing lessons, such as clarifying lesson aims with the students, ensuring students know the criteria for success and what they need to work on to improve, the ratings given by the teachers in this school, as in other schools in the project, bore no relationship to the observers' ratings of the extent to which these attributes were evident in the lessons. Using evidence is essential to the integrity of the process.

The visiting facilitator was careful to work with the teachers in ways that were both respectful and challenging. She did not sidestep their beliefs, but used tact and evidence to help them see that their beliefs and the practices on which they were based were not having the consequences they sought. In this way, she engaged their beliefs about teaching writing so the difference between them and what she proposed was clear to the teachers. As identified in Chapter 2, when there are discrepancies between existing and proposed practice, it is important to be explicit about these discrepancies to prevent problems of over-assimilation, where teachers interpret ideas within existing cognitive frameworks and so do not understand the fundamental differences between what is proposed and their current practice.

This case can be contrasted with one described by Cynthia Coburn[34] in California in which the state mandated that teachers take a whole language approach to their reading programmes. Coburn described how teachers' prior beliefs determined how they interpreted the key messages. The teachers who agreed with the messages sought further clarification and worked out ways to implement them. Those who disagreed with them found many reasons for why the approach would not work, usually focusing on the unrealistic premises of the policy for their particular students rather than challenge their existing beliefs. In both cases, teachers migrated to like-minded colleagues who reinforced prior theories.

The teachers in the writing case came to the situation with more openness to adopting an inquiry habit of mind than in the secondary school case on restorative justice. This starting point made the process faster and easier but inquiry habits of mind were developed through the problem-solving process in the restorative justice case. Both cases show the importance of having access to expert knowledge, building on this initial openness to learn in the one case and developing it in the other.

Deepening professional knowledge

Deepening professional knowledge and refining skills is funda-mental to change and improvement. That is why the cycle is labelled an inquiry and knowledge-building cycle; inquiry without new knowledge can result in process without substance. This is the heart of the inquiry cycle but, as I described above, it is not the beginning. The beginning is establishing learning needs. When teachers move directly into developing knowledge without establishing student and teacher learning needs, there is little evidence of changes in entrenched patterns of student engagement, learning and well-being, with two exceptions that we identified in the professional learning and development best evidence synthesis. The first exception is when teachers begin with a very low knowledge and skill base. Under these circumstances, providing teachers with clear guidelines and basic instructional techniques can be very helpful. The second exception is when the professional development targets very specific teaching skills in discrete areas. For example, changes in secondary students' map-reading skills and elementary students' phonemic awareness came after relatively short teacher engagement. There was no evidence of impact on achievement in geography or reading comprehension, however.

I am often asked about whether beginning with students is relevant to introducing new curriculum or responding to a new idea. Isn't it best to begin with what is new and deepen professional knowledge about that rather than start with students? My answer is that although what is 'new' might be the impetus for engaging in professional learning, it still needs to be examined in terms of the difference it is to make to students. What are the student engagement and learning issues that will be met through the introduction of the new curriculum? How will it be different for students than what happened before? By starting with students, their needs are kept to the forefront with the rationale for their learning retained.

At this stage in the cycle, important questions emerge around the kinds of knowledge that teachers need to develop and how they and others who are supporting their learning should proceed. Once again, the findings of John Bransford and colleagues on how people learn provide some insights.[35] Their first finding focused on the importance of engaging teachers' prior theories about teaching and learning and was introduced in Chapter 2. Their second finding focuses on the kinds of knowledge and skills required that I have adapted from a focus on students to a focus on teachers. These authors emphasize that to develop competence in an area of inquiry, teachers must have a deep foundation of factual knowledge, understand facts and ideas in the context of a conceptual framework, and organize knowledge in ways that facilitate their retrieval and application.

In teaching situations, developing competence requires both opportunities to develop the deep foundation of knowledge outside of the immediate demands of practice and opportunities to understand it within practice situations. Professional learning is not a process of learning new things and then learning how to implement them. Implementation is part of how something is learned and more deeply understood.[36] The teacher participating in the restorative justice programme who was surprised that she had to participate in a restorative conversation with the student after removing him from class is a case in point. Her understanding of restorative justice deepened through implementation to the point where she was able to readily retrieve and apply the ideas in principled ways. No amount of training external to the situation could have given her this kind of insight.

> **"**Professional learning is not a process of learning new things and then learning how to implement them. Implementation is part of how something is learned and more deeply understood.**"**

Knowledge for academic improvement

In academic areas, the professional learning and development best evidence synthesis showed us the kinds of foci for teacher learning that were associated with improvement in student outcomes. These foci were common to both primary and secondary school teachers and across curriculum areas. Regardless of whether the focus was mathematics, science, reading or writing, the emphasis was on knowledge of the subject and how that was evident in the curriculum, knowledge and skills of how to teach it, and how to assess what students knew and the progress they were making. It is over 20 years since Lee Shulman[37] described the specialized form of knowledge needed to teach effectively as 'pedagogical content knowledge' and it still forms the foundation of what it means to be a teacher. More recently, Judy Parr and I[38] found a strong relationship between a measure of teachers' pedagogical content knowledge in writing and students' progress within a given teacher's class.

Teaching can become more responsive to students' needs when the teacher understands what students already know and can do, and what misconceptions they hold. A seminal review by Paul Black and Dylan Wiliam in 1998 brought international attention to the power of this kind of formative assessment to accelerate students' learning and achievement.[39] More recent research has built on this work to show that involving students in assessment and shaping their learning goals can be even more powerful.[40] From this perspective, subject knowledge, pedagogical knowledge and assessment knowledge are not three forms of knowledge that sit separately; they are integrated and work hand in hand with one another. For example, a teacher might assess a group of students and find they have not understood a particular concept. Unless the teacher understands the concept deeply, he or she is unlikely to be able to analyse possible misconceptions and create alternative approaches to teaching it.

In the professional learning and development best evidence synthesis, some foci were found to be more important than others depending on teachers' existing knowledge and learning needs. For example, in primary schools, teachers' knowledge of reading tended to be stronger than in writing or mathematics, so greater attention was given to how texts and numbers work in the latter two areas than in reading. In secondary schools, teachers often attended professional development because they were teaching in subjects in which they had not undertaken university study. In these cases curriculum knowledge was emphasized but clearly had to go hand in hand with how it was taught and assessed.

Knowing about something in ways that it becomes organized into conceptual frameworks so that it can be readily retrieved, as John Bransford and colleagues[41] described, means knowing it both in theory and in practice. Teachers are always selecting particular teaching strategies moment by moment in classrooms. Making the right choices and being able to retrieve them and apply them requires an understanding of why one approach is better than another. The best evidence synthesis on professional learning and development identified that just knowing what teaching strategies were better, without a theoretical understanding of why they were better was not associated with the same gains in student outcomes. Part of the reason for this finding goes back to the problem of over-assimilation.

> "When the theory behind a strategy is poorly understood these adaptations are likely to be inconsistent with the theory underpinning them, and therefore, less effective."

Teachers inevitably adapt practices according to perceptions of their match to student needs and what they believe to be effective. Indeed, the use of formative assessment strategies requires that they do so. When the theory behind a strategy is poorly understood these adaptations are likely to be inconsistent with the theory underpinning them, and therefore, less effective. When the theory is well understood, the adaptations are more likely to become more responsive to students within a principled framework of practice.

Teaching is a complex, theoretically informed activity and the theories underpinning practices are inevitably personal. If personal theories are not deeply informed by wider knowledge about effectiveness and why things work, then teaching becomes a personal rather than a professional enterprise. Many teachers resist the need to understand theory because they perceive that their job is about practice. When they understand how theory informs practice and the two are intrinsically linked, they usually come to be more open to the possibility that theory really matters.

Conditions for developing deep knowledge

In both of the cases described earlier in this chapter the learning opportunities were co-constructed with the teachers working in partnership with the experts to identify what it was they needed to learn to be more effective. Content was not delivered to individuals who then learned or did not learn it. Learning how to change practice was supported in ways that were responsive to the teachers' learning needs. This did not mean that engagement was voluntary or options about change were left to individual teachers. What it meant was, given a specific problem with student outcomes, teachers had some control over the learning process. From the beginning, they discussed ideas, talked about their varying interpretations and used the conversations to shape their learning. Knowledge was co-constructed between the leader and the teachers, and among the teachers themselves.

We learned in the professional learning and development best evidence synthesis about the importance of constructing knowledge socially. In all situations associated with substantive improvement in student outcomes, teachers had opportunities to discuss important ideas within some kind of professional community of practice. Change was not a matter for individual reflection alone. As Lucas and Claxton[42] remind us, talent does not exist in isolation and systems change relies on developing social capital.

Learning is also not a one-off event, but rather a process of learning and change over time. A graduate student working with these ideas in British Columbia, Canada, expressed her experience as follows:

> The first of these ideas is that, for professional learning to truly take place, it should not be a one-day seminar or workshop. Just like students, teachers too need multiple opportunities to learn. Duh. I cannot think of a time in my teaching career that I have ever spent an entire lesson or day with students on a particular topic, and then never addressed that topic again. I have, however, spent a number of professional development days at workshops, seminars, or conferences and promptly forgot half of what I had learned. And, the half that I did remember, and maybe even implemented, slowly disappeared because I was never given any opportunity to talk about what I was doing with the learning, or hear of the successes or struggles of my colleagues.[43]

Many studies of professional learning and development focus on the activities and tasks involved in constructing these opportunities rather than what was learned. When searching for studies to include in the best evidence synthesis, we found studies that looked at lesson study, teacher coaching, demonstration of teaching practice, discussing practice with colleagues, and using assessment information to refine teaching. For every example of an activity associated with positive outcomes, we also found a counter-example. It was much more important that the activities were directly relevant to achieving the goals of professional learning and of building relevant knowledge and understanding of the ideas both theoretically and in practice than the form of the activity. Just as teachers are expected to make their lesson activities relevant to lesson aims and be flexible in what they provide for students, anyone who is providing professional learning opportunities should ensure their activities are relevant in the same way. Activities that are only indirectly related to learning aims, however engaging, do not achieve learning goals.

Professional learning activities do not need to be face to face. Many teachers use the internet to develop their knowledge and skills once they know what it is they need to learn. The description in the following case illustrates how written materials can serve as an important source of professional learning.

'Everyone knows what's next.'[44]

(Teacher in a special school)

The staff in this special school had a very good understanding of formative assessment practices. They regularly involved students in formulating their individual education plans, jointly identifying goals and deciding how they should be monitored. Engaging with effective formative assessment, however, raised new challenges. One challenge was to identify and describe exactly what students could do and their next learning steps in the kind of detail needed to teach these students effectively. Another was the length of time staff were taking to record this level of detail. Compounding both these challenges was the high turnover of teaching assistants who were responsible for much of the one-to-one work with students.

They decided to bring in expert assistance to help them develop progressions in learning in English and mathematics, particularly at pre-national curriculum levels. The developmental sequencing of mathematics, for example, was broken down into seven strands with each strand having detailed descriptions of specific stages within that strand. These descriptions formed a powerful learning tool for the students, teaching assistants and teachers. Any member of staff could pick up a student's folder, identify where a student was at according to the colour coded recording system, and find out what the student needed to know and do.

To achieve a system lift in student engagement, learning and well-being, professional learning opportunities need to be focused on just that – enhancing engagement, learning and well-being, with transparent expectations of learning and change. To get there, teachers need to be supported through a variety of relevant learning opportunities that are co-constructed with them to solve particular problems. Then the learning opportunities can occur both in situ where new practices are expected to be enacted and outside of these immediate situations to provide teachers with opportunities to discuss and reflect. Each complements the other and contributes to the learning and expectations of change.

Reflecting on your professional learning experiences

Think about the last time you led or participated in some kind of learning focused on building professional knowledge and skills.

Together with those with whom you worked, decide if your activities were at a basic, developing or integrated level using the descriptors below. What evidence do you have to support your decision? Do others have evidence that leads to a different decision?

Identifying professional learning needs

Basic	Developing	Integrated
The learning needs of the teachers were not made explicit or discussed. Engagement in professional learning began with presentation of new information	The learning needs of the teachers were linked to student learning needs but not systematically identified through an evidence-informed process to identify current beliefs and practices	The learning needs of the teachers were identified through a co-constructed evidence-informed process designed to identify teacher beliefs and practices linked to students' learning needs

Expectations of students

Basic	Developing	Integrated
Low student achievement and engagement was presented as a problem resting with students, not with teaching	Low student achievement and engagement was accepted as part of a teacher's responsibility but efforts to address them were individual and incidental to the professional learning	Low student achievement and engagement was presented as a teaching/learning/relationship issue that requires a systematic approach to professional learning

Integration of theory and practice

Basic	Developing	Integrated
Theory or practice was emphasized, but not both, with few opportunities for their integration	Reasons for particular practices were provided but considered separately. Practice situations were perceived as opportunities to apply theory	Theory and practice were fully integrated with opportunities to practice seen as opportunities to deepen theoretical understandings

If any of the activities were at a basic or developing level, decide together what each of you needs to do to move them towards becoming more integrated. What evidence might you collect to monitor if your activities are moving closer to the description at the integrated level? Decide when you will check your progress and how you will do it.

4

Checking New
Opportunities for Students

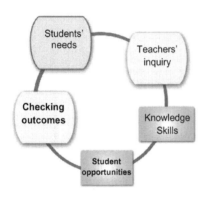

The ultimate goal of teacher learning is change in teaching practices that make a difference for students. With this in mind, the final two dimensions of the inquiry and knowledge-building cycle involve checking that teachers' participation in professional learning activities has resulted in new opportunities for students to improve their engagement, learning and well-being. The checking dimensions involve finding out what is changed in students' learning environments and in the outcomes that were the original reason for teachers to participate. This checking process is an important part of the inquiry and knowledge-building cycle to ensure the teachers' participation has actually resulted in changes to practice in ways that enhance those student outcomes of focus. The process also contributes to deepening professional learning by examining practice and identifying what needs to be refocused to make further improvements.

Checking is important because teaching and learning are complex processes. There is no straight line between professional learning opportunities, changes to practice and changes to student outcomes. In the early research that identified the importance of formative assessment on student learning, Black and Wiliam[45] used the term 'black boxes' to depict the unpredictable impact of particular acts of teaching on student learning. The relationship between teaching inputs and student learning can never be assured because *how* students interpret and use the available understandings and skills influences *what* they learn. Much depends on students' prior knowledge and motivation. Identifying the impact of professional learning experiences on student outcomes is even more demanding because there is a second black box. The influence of professional learning on teaching depends on how teachers interpret the understandings and use the particular skills made available through the professional learning opportunities. Much depends on their prior knowledge and professional orientations. Any changes in teaching practice will have variable consequences for student outcomes. Figure 4.1 illustrates the parallels and processes for teachers and students.

There can also be variability in changes to classroom practice and student outcomes if teachers do not see that engaging in professional learning necessarily means making changes to practice. Deidre Le Fevre[46] interviewed teachers involved in professional development in a school reform initiative and found they rarely referred to making changes. Learning was not necessarily perceived as meaning that they should change something. Many of their leaders expressed frustration with the lack of change. Not much is

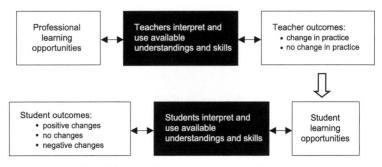

Figure 4.1 The black boxes of teacher and student learning

likely to happen for students unless changing practice is seen as an integral part of teacher learning.

Checking that students have new opportunities to learn is also a way to deepen teachers' professional understandings and to identify what needs to be refocused and refined to continue improvements. From this perspective, monitoring practice and its impact on students is not checking that teachers are complying with requirements to practice in new ways but rather finding out what else needs to be learned. Through trying things out in practice and checking to see if students are responding differently, learning is deepened. It is here that the third of the findings of John Bransford and colleagues from the National Research Council[47] on how people learn is applicable. I mentioned their first two findings earlier – the importance of engaging prior beliefs and developing deep factual knowledge organized into conceptual frameworks. This third finding relates to learners becoming

> ❝The influence of professional learning on teaching depends on how teachers interpret the understandings and use the particular skills made available through the professional learning opportunities.❞

meta-cognitive and self-regulated through developing their own learning goals and monitoring their own effectiveness. Learning goals are developed early in the inquiry and knowledge-building cycle when teachers identify what they as teachers and their students need to learn (see Chapter 3). In the two dimensions that are the focus of this chapter, the goals become refined through an iterative process of monitoring effectiveness and making adjustments. For this reason, the questions in the inquiry and knowledge-building cycle have 'we' and 'our' as their referent instead of 'they' and 'their'. What knowledge and skills do *we* need? What has been the impact of *our* changed actions?

> ❝Through meta-cognitive and self-regulated learning processes, teachers come to take more control of their own learning. They are able to work in partnership with others who have specialist expertise to identify what is working well so it can be retained and what is not working so well in order to change.❞

Through these meta-cognitive and self-regulated learning processes, teachers come to take more control of their own learning. They are able to work in partnership with others who have specialist expertise to identify what is working well so it can be retained and what is not working so well in order to change it. If minor tweaking is required, it becomes part of the same cycle. When they need more substantive deepening of the focus for new learning, they can move to refocusing for the next cycle of inquiry, as indicated by the arrows in Figure 1.1. Engagement in one cycle of inquiry and knowledge-building is not usually sufficient for it to become a habitual way of thinking and acting. Nor is it sufficient to solve entrenched problems of teaching and learning.

In the remainder of this chapter I unpack these final two dimensions of the inquiry cycle: engaging students in new learning experiences and checking the impact of changed actions on valued outcomes for students. The four components identified in Figure 2.1 for evidence-informed conversations once again make up the important components within each dimension: having relevant evidence, developing an inquiry habit of mind, building relationships of respect and challenge, and accessing expert knowledge. I conclude with a comment on refocusing for the next cycle of inquiry.

Engaging students in new learning experiences

Clearly, something needs to change for students within their learning environments if outcomes related to their engagement, learning or well-being are to improve. The teachers as learners and those facilitating their learning have a dual challenge. They need to check whether or not appropriate change is occurring in students' opportunities to learn. They also need to do this checking in ways that promote further professional learning and change rather than undermining them. There are no easy answers to either challenge.

Observation of classroom practice, or of other relevant contexts, is the obvious mechanism for finding out if things have changed in students' learning environments. But like many obvious answers, it is not straightforward in reality. Classrooms are complex places with multiple teaching/learning interactions occurring at once and it is difficult to determine what should be observed and how to decide. I have identified a few important principles to guide this decision-making.

First, what is observed relates directly to the professional learning area of focus and includes teachers' learning goals that have been developed to address a specific problem of practice. Second, the focus should be jointly decided by the observer and the person being observed. Learning partnerships should not have unpleasant surprises associated with them. Third, the criteria for determining what constitutes effectiveness are determined through references to the research and professional literature agreed in advance by the observer and the person being observed. Having a learning partnership means everyone is on the same page as far as possible with the partners drawing on the best sources of information available.

Included in the criteria should be whether students are responding differently because this must be the main arbiter for determining effectiveness. An example of why this is important is described by Adrienne Alton-Lee and colleagues.[48] They reported how teachers jointly planned social studies lessons aimed to reduce racism. When they recorded the students' conversations, they found that one teacher inadvertently increased opportunities for racist comments to minority students through the language he used in the lesson. Thus, his approach led to greater marginalization of these students than before. Finally, what is observed then becomes the focus of a professional learning conversation designed to deepen understanding of the criteria in practice and refine teaching skills. An example of such a conversation and the principles underpinning it is provided in Chapter 6.

The difference between an observation of practice that promotes learning and one that is primarily about compliance can be subtle. I have tried to illustrate some nuances of the principles in the following cases – one that was successful and then a contrasting one that was less successful.[49]

'Would you like me to observe you or would you like me to have a go while you watch me?'

(Team leader)

The teachers of six-year-old students in a school located in a low socio-economic community had participated in intensive literacy professional development for more than a year with teachers from other schools in their community. Their learning goals were focused on solving teaching/ learning problems with low progress students. The students' reading progress was carefully monitored at a team meeting every school term to ensure they were on a trajectory to reach the standard by the end of their first year at school. Nearly all students were keeping up with expectations with a steady improvement evident over time but three girls in one teacher's class were falling behind. She brought the team's attention to these students with the comment that she could not seem to move them through the book levels. They were not retaining the vocabulary needed for the next level and she asked for the assistance of the team.

By this time in the team's development, shared criteria for both teaching practices and what counted as student success had been established and the teacher was able to anticipate the kinds of questions the team would ask her. She had undertaken a detailed diagnosis of the students' reading vocabulary and reading strategies. Indeed, the questions she had anticipated were asked but it seemed to her that the suggested solutions would not help her or the students. The team leader concluded that new information and possibly a new lens needed to be brought to bear on the problem, so she asked the teacher, *'Would you like me to observe you or would you like me to have a go while you watch me?'* The teacher responded by asking the team leader to observe her teaching the class. Time release was organized and the observation began with the leader observing the teacher but ended up with the leader working directly with the students and trying different approaches herself. The students began to respond more positively to some of the leader's strategies so their discussion following the lesson focused on the reasons why this might have been the case and what the teacher could try. The essence of their discussion was reported back to the team at their next meeting.

In contrast, achievement in one of the other schools involved in the same professional development was not improving. The process for their observations met some of the principles outlined above but not others. Their observations were focused on what they had learned in the professional development and they planned the criteria together. Despite this, the teachers were negative and viewed the observations as a compliance exercise rather than a learning one. The leader had not disclosed that her reasons for undertaking the observations were her concern that the teachers were not implementing the practices promoted in the professional development well. Rather, she indicated that the observations were to find out how things were going in a general sense. The criteria they developed were focused on teaching practices and omitted how the students were responding to those practices. The teachers were learning to teach (perform) correctly, rather than to teach in ways that solved teaching/learning problems. The leader believed that the teachers would feel threatened if they received individual feedback because many were not implementing the strategies promoted in the professional development. She did not want to put them on the spot so collated the records from all the observations and reported the collated findings at the next team meeting. The teachers distanced themselves from the generic feedback perceiving that it applied to others rather than themselves. The conversation reverted to discussing how overwhelming the difficulties were in teaching students from low socio-economic communities.

Evidence-informed conversations
about new learning opportunities

Observations provide evidence of individual or school-wide practices. School-wide observations using consistent criteria allow teachers and leaders to obtain profiles across a whole school and thus provide a picture on which to base professional learning foci. With guidance, teachers can then discuss the profiles to help work their focus for learning. This approach might be important in the early stages to develop collective understandings and focus.

Through identifying the criteria for effective practice together and discussing the findings from the observations, these discussions can deepen collective understandings of particular practices, especially if students' responses form part of the criteria. As the contrasting cases illustrated, however, if the observations are school-wide, teachers must perceive that the evidence is directly relevant to them and their practice.

The two cases described above show a contrast in the other components of evidence-informed conversations of developing an inquiry habit of mind, relationships of respect and challenge, and accessing expert knowledge (Figure 2.1). Inquiry habits of mind were more evident in the first case where the teachers were actively searching to solve teaching/learning problems, than in the contrasting case in which they were not seeking to learn or change. The two schools had been engaged in the professional development for the same amount of time.[50] The difference resulted from the way in which the leaders approached their within-school learning tasks and how they interpreted relationships of respect and challenge. In the first case, the leader had a strong sense of urgency about solving the students' underachievement problem and expected the teachers to join her in this task. Her actions and the reasons for them were transparent. Nothing was hidden. Relationships were highly respectful in that she treated the teachers as professionals who together were learning to solve a problem they all shared. High levels of challenge were an accepted part of the task. In the contrasting case, the leader showed respect to the teachers by protecting them from her concerns. She did not disclose her real reasons for the observations so had difficulty challenging them about their practices in respectful ways when the observations found them to be problematic. As a result the teachers disregarded the information and reverted to their previous perceptions that the students were the problem.

Both groups had similar access to external expertise and had engaged in the same professional development. The teachers in the first case, however, were developing their collective knowledge further through their problem-solving efforts. In the contrasting case the within-school activities failed to develop their knowledge beyond what had been presented in the professional development sessions themselves. Independently conducted research observations in each school showed that adaptations to the approach advocated in the professional development had been made in both schools. In the first school, these adaptations were consistent with the theoretical underpinnings of the approach originally presented. When the researcher discussed the process involved in making the adaptations the teachers described a deliberate process of trialling and checking with the leader when specific students did not make adequate progress. In the contrast case, adaptations were also justified in terms of students' needs, but these were perceived generic needs that were not systematically checked. In reality, the adaptations consisted mostly of returning to teaching practices used prior to their involvement in the professional development. These contrasting cases of adaptations underline the idea that knowing about practice means knowing the theory underpinning it. It is important to know why it works.

Checking impact on students

Checking outcomes for students ensures that teachers' participation in professional learning actually results in the desired improvement in student outcomes. It also allows teachers to deepen their learning about the area of focus and identify what students need next so that teachers can move forward through further iterations of the inquiry and knowledge-building cycle. At this stage, teachers should ask themselves the following questions.

> **"Checking outcomes for students ensures that teachers' participation in professional learning actually results in the desired improvement in student outcomes."**

- How effective has what we have learned and done been in promoting our students' learning?
- What should we keep going? What should we refine? What should we stop?
- What new student learning challenges have become evident so what more do we need to learn?

Asking and answering these questions can happen on a lesson-by-lesson basis or over a longer term. Longer-term cycles should be more formal and deliberate, with systematic building of knowledge being the reason that teachers engage in the process. The case described earlier in the chapter about problem-solving observations showed how the cycle worked among a group of committed teachers and leaders through one kind of formal process. Others might involve external experts. The case described below shows a more informal process. Aspects of this case were described in Chapter 3. Teachers were identifying what they needed to learn to improve their students' writing in a small primary school. The case began with the quote, 'Now we know why they didn't get it'.

More details on how the teachers began to check on the impact of their practice on students and the surprises they encountered are described below.

'We found they still didn't get it, so we had to be even clearer.'

(Teacher)

At the time of the classroom observations, the visiting facilitator interviewed the students who had difficulty describing the lesson aims or the specific features of the writing purpose that would make it effective. As a result of working with the professional learning facilitator, the teachers felt more confident in expressing the lesson aims to the students and constructing criteria for success with them so that the students had a vision of the features of effective recounts which was the main writing purpose on which they were working. They decided to assess if the changes they had made now meant things were clearer for the students so they decided to interview the students themselves during the writing lessons using the same questions the facilitator had used earlier. These questions asked:

What are you working on today? (General introduction to get the students talking)

What are you learning about writing recounts while you are doing this? (To find out students' understanding of the lesson aims)

Can you tell me what a good recount looks like? (To find out if students know the criteria for success)

Who are you writing this recount for? (To find out if students are writing for an audience)

What are you working on to improve your writing? (Understanding of feedback/feed forward for next steps)

Despite the teachers believing they were much clearer about their lesson aims and criteria for success, they were surprised to find that many of the students' answers to the questions were little better than they were before they had made the changes in their writing lessons. They discussed this problem at their next meeting and decided that they needed to be even more explicit with the students. They tried again being clearer about what they wanted the students to learn and what success looked like. This time they had much greater success. They noticed also that the students appeared to be more motivated to engage in writing as they became clearer about the purpose and what they were supposed to be learning.

Evidence-informed conversations about student outcomes

So what is involved in checking impact on students? Once again, the themes of using relevant evidence, developing an inquiry habit of mind, building relationships of trust and challenge, and accessing expert knowledge help to unpack the cases in this chapter. Teachers must see the assessment information that they are using to assess impact as relevant to their professional learning. When teachers are used to collecting data on students for grading or reporting, as noted in Chapter 2, they are likely to revert quickly to these external purposes, especially if the changes they have made have not been particularly successful in improving the outcomes on which they were focused. It is a significant shift in thinking to use the assessment information to assist the teachers to reflect back on what went right, what went wrong, and to orient them to what else they should try. This shift is essential to maintaining a learning orientation. What is the evidence for improvement? What are the gaps? What are the misconceptions that need correcting? Engaging in shorter checking cycles as described in the second case can help to prevent unpleasant surprises over a longer term.

Using fit-for-purpose assessment tasks applies as much at this point in the cycle as it did earlier. Delving into students' understanding of their learning provides immediate feedback to teachers about their next teaching moves. It is also important to assess progress over the longer term, such as a year or more, with more standardized evidence to ensure that the students' progress is adequate. Using comparable assessments to those that were used at the beginning of the cycle allows for a more robust assessment of progress to be made than using different tools. It may be that with improvement in teachers' knowledge the original tools will now be considered inadequate, but it is important to maintain some kind of comparability. An additional consideration at this point in the cycle is to search for unintended consequences. What else might be going on? Do you have hunches that something else may be suffering through focusing on a specific area? Is it possible that achievement is rising but motivation is declining? The information collected needs to embrace alternative possibilities as well as the main focus.

The quality of the ensuing discussions relies as much on developing an inquiry habit of mind, relationships of respect and challenge, and access to relevant expertise as it does to the actual data. Inquiry habits of mind can be developed through examining the assessment information if the surrounding discussions are treated by those leading them as a learning opportunity and conducting the discussions in respectful and challenging ways. Blame and shame are counterproductive to promoting learning. What areas and which students have shown improvement? Is the improvement adequate? What areas and which students have not shown improvement?

One of the most contested issues around interpretation comes when people try to identify possible causes of improvement or non-improvement. Investigating possible causes is fundamental to promoting an inquiry habit of mind and further learning. This process is aided greatly by bringing together evidence of changes in teaching practice and evidence of student learning. By doing so, the group can investigate possible causes over which teachers have some control.

Often in discussions about assessment information, interpretation is left to individual musings and not discussed. As described in Chapter 2, the assessment information does not speak for itself. It is important to check the lens individuals are bringing to interpretation, particularly when it comes to exploring possible causes for things not having gone as well as was hoped. Identifying causes depends on personal theories and it is quite possible that there are as many different theories as people in the room with problems seen as being someone else's responsibility. When interpretations are held up to scrutiny through disclosure and discussion, people are more likely to consider their own actions in the causal mix. Once again, questions like the following are important scaffolds for moving forward. 'How effective has what we have learned and done been in promoting our students' learning?', 'What should we continue?', 'What should we refine?' and 'What should we stop?'

Throughout this discussion of causation, I have used words such as 'possible causes' and 'exploring causes' because it is rare to be able to establish causation with any precision. Many factors contribute to student engagement, learning and well-being, not just teaching. There are black boxes, not straight lines, linking one to the other. Researchers and practitioners are gradually unpacking these black boxes and it is increasingly apparent that teachers can have a strong influence on outcomes for students.

External expertise is often the catalyst that teachers need during the interpretation process to shift the conversation from blaming others to thinking about what they can change. External experts can bring new lens to the interpretation process and can also help challenge existing social norms within groups, especially where those norms are directed to reinforcing rather than challenging the status quo. The contrasting case at the beginning of this chapter in which teachers were not implementing new practices and attributed the students' lack of progress to their backgrounds is a case in point. Through a researcher attending the meetings and

> "External experts can bring new lens to the interpretation process and can also help challenge existing social norms within groups, especially where those norms are directed to reinforcing rather than challenging the status quo."

bringing attention to the processes that were happening, the leader was able to change her way of working. Revisiting the team a year later showed more productive team norms where the reason for particular actions was made transparent and there was no mention of difficult students who were impossible to teach.[51]

Teachers as adaptive experts

The first case presented in Chapter 2 is typical of what happens when teachers engage in iterative cycles of inquiry with the assistance of experts in a particular curriculum area. In this case the focus of teacher learning evolved from a generic one of 'reading', to paragraph comprehension, to vocabulary and finally to metaphorical and colloquial vocabulary before they solved the achievement problem. As the teachers learned more about assessing students and developed their pedagogical content knowledge further, they were able to analyse students' needs more deeply and understand what they needed to learn to meet those needs.

A similar process has been evident in all the other cases described so far, whether they have focused on student suspensions or on writing. The process has involved refocusing on particular needs or on particular groups of students. Once teachers have developed inquiry habits of mind underpinning the inquiry and knowledge-building cycle, they are constantly asking themselves 'What new challenges have become evident?' 'So what more do we need to learn?'

The knowledge and skills involved, together with the disposition to inquire, come together in the image of the teacher as an adaptive expert. The image was originally proposed by Hatano and Inagaki[52] and further developed by others[53] from the United States. In a more elaborated version presented here, I suggest that adaptive experts are deeply knowledgeable about both the content of what is taught and how to teach it. They are aware of their assumptions underpinning their practice and know when they are helpful and when to question them and if necessary to let them go. They become expert in retrieving, organizing and applying professional knowledge in light of the challenges and needs presented by the students they are teaching. The routines involve being constantly vigilant about the impact of their teaching on students' engagement, learning and well-being. To exercise this vigilance, they also know how to assess students on relevant attributes over both short and long time frames. What may appear to be working in the immediate situation may not be as effective over time. They have the capability to work out when known routines do not work and sufficient knowledge to work out innovative approaches when needed. Part of being an adaptive expert is to know when and from where to seek help. Engaging in inquiry and knowledge-building cycles is at the core of their professionalism.

Reflecting on your professional learning experiences

Think about the last time you organized or engaged in some kind of analysis of teaching practice or student assessment information after making changes to practice as part of your professional learning. Together with those with whom you worked, decide if your activities were at a basic, developing or integrated level using the descriptors below. What evidence do you have to support your decision? Do others have evidence that leads to a different decision?

If you have never examined teaching practice or student assessment information after making changes to practice, use the descriptors below to think about where you could start.

Classroom observations

Basic	Developing	Integrated
Focus of observations is in the area of professional learning but other principles identified in the description for 'integrated' are largely absent	Focus of observations is jointly developed using agreed criteria for effectiveness. Student responses are not necessarily included. Follow-up conversations focus on superficial change	Focus of observations is jointly developed and incorporates teacher learning goals using agreed criteria for effectiveness including student responses. Follow-up conversations deepen understandings and areas for change

Assessing impact on students

Basic	Developing	Integrated
Only formal or informal assessment of student learning is used. No reference is made to teaching practice during the interpretation process	Formal assessment information is combined with informal information. Anecdotal information on teaching practice is used during the interpretation process	Formal assessment information is combined with informal information. Systematic information on teaching practice is used as an integral part of the interpretation process

Refocusing the next iteration of the inquiry and knowledge-building cycle

Basic	Developing	Integrated
Further engagement in the cycle is left to teachers to decide focus without specific challenges to the status quo	Further engagement in the cycle is expected but remains at a similar level rather than going deeper. External expertise may be engaged but does not challenge the status quo sufficiently to go deeper	Further engagement in the cycle is constantly challenging existing assumptions and developing new knowledge and skills. Going deeper is an integral part of further development

If any of the activities were at a basic or developing level, decide together what each of you needs to do to move them towards becoming more integrated. What evidence might you collect to monitor if your activities are moving closer to the description at the integrated level? Decide when you will check your progress and how you will do it.

5

School Leaders as
Leaders of Learning

My emphasis on teachers
in this book so far reflects
how important teaching
is to making a difference
for students. Teachers and
students form the core of
work in schools.[54] Teachers
alone, however, cannot
be expected to solve the
urgent problems facing

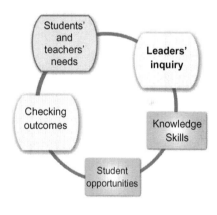

many schools and the students who attend them. Learning how to
do things differently is difficult and depends on teachers receiving
systematic support from school leaders within their everyday working
environments. Professional learning that is disconnected from
these everyday situations rarely makes much difference to students
who show limited engagement, have difficulty understanding what
they need to learn, and do not see school as a psychologically
safe place to be.

There is a large research literature on school leadership but only recently has this research begun to focus on the kinds of leadership that make a difference to outcomes for students. One of the reasons is that measuring the impact of leaders is more difficult than for teachers because leaders' influence is more indirect. It occurs mostly through teachers but is still very important. Viviane Robinson and colleagues[55] recently identified five leadership dimensions associated with higher than expected student achievement, through a meta-analysis of the research. Their results are summarized in Figure 5.1. Four dimensions with a moderate impact include establishing goals and expectations; resourcing strategically; planning, co-ordinating and evaluating teaching and the curriculum; and ensuring an orderly and supportive environment. The dimension with twice the

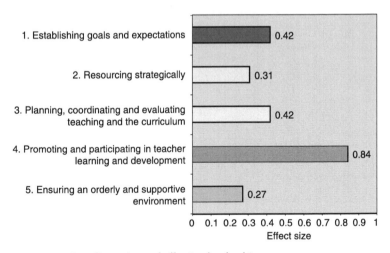

Figure 5.1 Five dimensions of effective leadership.
Source: Adapted from Robinson, V., Hohepa, M. and Lloyd, C. (2009). *School Leadership and Student Outcomes: Identifying What Works and Why: A Best Evidence Synthesis.* Wellington: Ministry of Education.

effect size of others involves leaders promoting and participating in teacher learning and development. Clearly, when leaders make a difference to what teachers learn, it makes a difference for students.

The idea of leaders within schools taking on learning-focused roles for their teachers is not new[56] but it does mean moving beyond traditional views of school leadership that have usually focused on personal traits, tasks and relationships. Linda Kaser and Judy Halbert[57] propose new leadership mindsets if schools are to move from sorting students to promoting their learning, which in many ways resonates with the essence of the messages in this book. These mindsets include an intense moral purpose focused on promoting deep student learning, professional inquiry, trusting relationships, and seeking evidence in action. They propose that a key leadership mindset is creating a learning-oriented design in schools that reflects the complexity required to create appropriate conditions, structures and rhythms for professional learning. Mindsets are not about picking up a few pointers here and there, but about seeing and doing things in new ways. As teachers must see things in new ways if all students are to engage and achieve, so must their leaders.

> "A key leadership mindset is creating a learning-oriented design in schools that reflects the complexity required to create appropriate conditions, structures and rhythms for professional learning."

Given the focus of this book, this chapter is unapologetically about leadership that creates learning-oriented designs for teachers in ways that make a difference for students. In taking this focus I also acknowledge that effective leaders do many other things to keep their schools functioning well, such as organizing and managing resources, and working with people other than teachers including parents, communities, district and local offices. Important as these other roles are, this book is not about them, but about promoting learning throughout the school.

This chapter begins by identifying who the leaders responsible for professional learning might be in a school and how they can exercise their learning leadership roles. The next section focuses on what these leaders need to know and do to create professional learning environments that are consistent with mindsets focused on promoting student engagement, learning and well-being. This description draws on a study of five principals who were highly effective in raising their students' literacy achievement and other work related to the leadership of learning. I describe some of the specific challenges these leaders faced and how they approached their own professional learning through adapting the teachers' inquiry and knowledge-building cycle to meet their own leadership learning needs. The chapter concludes by identifying what it means to develop leadership and organizational adaptive expertise in ways that parallel the earlier discussion of teachers as adaptive experts.

Identifying the leaders of learning

In organizational diagrams, the principal or head is the designated leader of schools. In reality, the complexities involved in schooling mean that leadership is distributed across different people and situations. Jim Spillane's[58] ground-breaking take on this work in this area challenged the idea that leadership rests with a particular person and demonstrated that leadership is more like patterns of influence distributed across many players. Leadership effectiveness as I think of it in this book depends on how this influence promotes leader and teacher learning (and in many cases parent learning) in ways that improves the engagement, learning and well-being of all students. This is not the work of one person.

Understanding leadership as being distributed across people does not mean that the principal or head teacher delegates responsibility to others and remains aloof from what is happening in students' learning environments. Rather it means exercising influence through many different leadership practices to maximize learning for all. These practices involve interacting with teachers and developing relevant materials, routines and structures to promote learning. Sometimes the leader is not physically present. For example, materials might involve providing teachers with student profiles of achievement in ways that clearly identify who is falling below the agreed standard in a particular curriculum area. Structures and routines may involve setting scheduled meetings for staff from a subject department to discuss how to assist these students. The specifics of how the materials, routines and structures are configured depend on the size and level of the school and the particular expertise of the teachers and leaders. The important principles, however, remain the same. I elaborate on them in the following sections of this chapter.

Leadership that promotes learning

The central challenge faced by all leaders is to create situations that promote teacher learning about teaching practices that make a difference for students. A study I undertook of five primary school principals, whose student literacy achievement on average improved 3.5 times the expected annual rate of progress, helped to clarify how effective leaders accomplished this.[59] I asked these principals to record situations where they considered that they were acting as

> ❝The central challenge faced by all leaders is to create situations that promote teacher learning about teaching practices that make a difference for students.❞

effective leaders of learning. The recordings were followed up with interviews of teachers, other leaders and themselves. The situations these principals chose all involved the fourth of Viviane Robinson and colleagues' dimensions of leadership that makes a difference for students; that of promoting and participating in teacher learning and development (Figure 5.1). Closer scrutiny of what they actually did, however, showed they were much more active than simply promoting learning. They *led* teacher learning and created school communities that learned. They did not neglect the other dimensions identified in Figure 5.1. I found this out by asking their teachers to rate how well their principals undertook these dimensions and the teachers rated them all very highly. What the leaders admitted to neglecting were some administrative tasks they believed did not contribute to student learning. They delegated these tasks to others.

The practices that were apparent in these leaders' recordings were the ways they led their teachers through inquiry and knowledge-building cycles by holding evidence-informed conversations with their teachers in ways that were consistent with the qualities in Figure 2.1. They brought a range of relevant evidence to their conversations. They accessed expert knowledge so both they and their teachers learned important knowledge and skills. They demonstrated and systematically developed inquiry habits of mind throughout their schools and showed relationships of respect and challenge. For this reason, this chapter is organized around these four qualities which are drawn together into a leadership inquiry and knowledge-building cycle.

Using relevant evidence

All the principals integrated two kinds of evidence in the situations they recorded: evidence about student learning and evidence about teaching practices that related directly to the aspects of student learning being discussed. Students were not talked about independently of how to teach them. Teaching was not talked about independently of its impact on students. These principals integrated both these kinds of evidence in ways that helped teachers to make the inquiry and knowledge-building cycle core to their work. The next case shows how one principal used evidence to challenge the thinking of two grade four teachers about writing.

'The students did quite well in reading and completely bombed out in writing and I am fascinated to know why.'

(School principal)

This principal regularly checked the students' achievement profiles and discovered that a group of grade four students had achieved well in reading but poorly in writing. He began the meeting with the quote in the heading for this case. He wanted to understand what the teachers thought. They explained that the students had started the year with low writing achievement and so the results did not surprise them. Rather than accept this explanation, he kept bringing the discussion back to the students' work, the focus of the teachers' programmes, and the reasons why they had adopted the particular programme focus for this group of students. It became clear that the teaching programme was not sufficiently targeted to meet these students' needs.

The discussion deepened and the principal contributed some ideas that the teachers could use to address the specific needs of these students with the teachers agreeing they could try. The principal was careful to check at each stage of the conversation that he was correctly interpreting what the teachers were saying and that they understood what he was suggesting. They agreed to meet again with evidence of the students' new writing efforts to see if they understood better what they needed to do.

During the follow-up interviews the teachers indicated that they did not feel they were being checked up on by the principal, but rather talked about how much they respected him for his deep knowledge of literacy and his commitment to all students' learning.

Accessing expert knowledge

Building knowledge is central to the inquiry cycle and accessing expert knowledge is central to this process. Inquiry without new knowledge can become a process of recycling what is already known and is unlikely to make a difference to the difficult problems of teaching and learning. Lorna Earl and Lynne Hannay[60] advocate that knowledge work becomes the core business of school leaders. As the case above describes, the leader in this school was a knowledge leader. He was not alone. All the leaders in this study took on this role. Their approach to building knowledge was to help teachers learn how to diagnose the learning needs of individual students and how to teach them in very specific ways, together with finding out why particular approaches and strategies were more likely to work than others. As a team, their approaches did not build knowledge in the abstract; it was very specific to the students and the task at hand. At the same time, they ensured that the knowledge was developed in ways that teachers could use it with other students and situations.

The question immediately arises about what leaders need to know if they are to take a leadership role in this knowledge-building process. These leaders were clear that as primary school heads they needed to know about teaching literacy and numeracy. They also took a distributed leadership approach and involved leaders in middle-management positions in developing similar levels of knowledge. In other areas they were relaxed about leaving the specialist knowledge to others and they took more of a support role. The next case provides a snapshot of how one of these leaders created situations to build her knowledge and that of the literacy curriculum leader, so they could become a source of expert knowledge for the teachers. Mostly, I have used her words.

'But this is our job isn't it?'[61]

(Principal)

This primary school was located in a community with very limited financial resources. The school was receiving state assistance to help them improve their low literacy achievement. A professional learning facilitator visited them approximately once every two weeks. The head considered that deep knowledge of literacy was central to her role so that she could be a leader of literacy for the teachers and students. She described one instance as an example of how she had recently created learning opportunities for the teachers, the literacy curriculum leader and herself.

> ...one of the things in the last round of classroom observations that seemed to be quite consistent is that the teachers are still not clear on how to form a learning intention [goal] using student data and how to work with the students to construct success criteria. I think it is a lot to do with their content knowledge and understanding that sequence and progression of learning. So we [professional learning facilitator, principal and literacy leader] decided to create a series of learning intentions for particular things that staff can go and put their hands on. So we continue the learning around the content knowledge in staff meetings, but actually I don't think we can afford to have one more day, one more week of children getting confused messages about learning intentions. So I'm hoping if we can create this kind of rubric that will show progressions in learning intentions and how to use the data, then the benefit will be the teachers can see the links and the progressions and use them. So we are going to try and make a complex task a little bit easier, but at the same time really develop the teachers' content knowledge around the reading process through going over the rubrics in the staff

> meeting as well. We can't do this by ourselves but working with [professional learning facilitator], we'll work it out. So when we're in classrooms we'll all know what we're looking for.

For this principal, and others in the study, the strong driver was to improve outcomes for students, not to create better teaching and learning in a generic sense. She described how she juggled the limitations of teachers' current knowledge with the need to accelerate the students' learning. By providing the teachers with progressions in learning intentions and using them to build teachers' content knowledge, she was able to achieve both at the same time. She scaffolded and constructed the teachers' learning in ways that enabled them to teach their classes of students in new ways. She accessed the expertise of the professional learning facilitator to allow her to carry out her responsibility as a knowledge leader and included the literacy curriculum leader so they both had sufficient expertise to work with the teachers.

Part of tuning into the rhythms for professional learning involved building the theory and practice together. She used the progressions of learning intentions created for use in classrooms as a platform for building further knowledge. It was not a theory into practice sequence but theory (what she referred to as 'content') and practice building together. When professional learning is focused on cycles of inquiry into students' needs, then making changes in students' learning environments becomes an integral part of building knowledge.

> "Part of tuning into the rhythms for professional learning involves building the theory and practice together."

In the introduction to this chapter I indicated that leadership for learning involves more than face-to-face interactions with teachers, it also includes the use of materials, routines and structures. These all influence what people learn and do. Materials are sometimes referred to as 'tools', the physical resources that help people learn more about doing their job. Effective tools convey knowledge about what is involved in a particular task and are sometimes referred to as smart tools.[62] In the case above, the learning intentions were smart tools because they conveyed several types of knowledge including the idea that learning intentions should be matched to student data and that they should be graduated according to students' progress on particular literacy tasks.

What was particularly important in this school was that developing this knowledge through the tool was integrated into the school routines. The leader expected teachers to use students' assessment profiles to develop learning intentions. This practice was part of the school's routines but poorly executed. By constructing the progression of learning intentions and using them in staff meetings she helped teachers both to improve the poorly executed routines of using students' assessment profiles to develop learning intentions and to develop the teachers' content knowledge around the reading process. In order to accomplish these two tasks through the tool, the leader identified that she needed to learn new things herself. Learning became both systematic and systemic.

The staff in this school, and in all the other schools, viewed their leaders as having expert knowledge both in theory and in practice. They were also aware that their leaders were actively searching for knowledge to further their learning. As described in the case above, the principal did not pretend that she knew how to write learning intentions encompassing detailed progressions in reading. Rather, she was aware of the need to do so and used the professional learning facilitator strategically to develop her expertise so she could assist her teachers. Leadership learning, like that of the staff, was deeply rooted in student learning.

Developing inquiry habits of mind

When leaders and teachers engage in ongoing inquiry and knowledge-building cycles, inquiry habits of mind become part of how things are done. Lorna Earl and Stephen Katz[63] describe these as habits of using inquiry and reflection to think about where you are, where you are going, and how you will get there, and then turning around to rethink the whole process to see how well it is working and make adjustments. What was clear in the recorded activities of the principals participating in the study was that they expected all their teachers to approach teaching-learning challenges with inquiry habits of mind.

This meant that these schools formed coherent inquiry and learning systems. The systems were focused but sufficiently flexible to meet individual teacher and student needs as they were identified. Opportunities for professional learning reflected the structure and rhythms of what typically happened throughout the school day, week and year.[64] Some were formal, others informal. Some were whole school and out-of-class. Others were individualized and situated within student learning environments. All moved in the same direction.

This coherence across professional learning environments was not achieved through the completion of checklists and scripted lessons but rather through creating learning situations that promoted inquiry habits of mind throughout the school. The specifics of literacy teaching were not prescribed but learned through ongoing analysis and discussion of teaching–learning relationships. Classroom-based help was always on hand for those teachers whose students were having difficulty making expected gains.

Inquiry habits of mind are underpinned by high expectations of leaders, teachers and students to learn and change. The principals explicitly positioned themselves as inquirers and learners and respected the capacity of their teachers to inquire into their practice for improvement purposes. No one was let off the hook. When the leaders talked to teachers about students not making sufficient progress they did so using statements and inquiry questions like, 'We need to rethink what we are doing' and 'How can we find out what will make a difference?'

> "Coherence across professional learning environments was not achieved through the completion of checklists and scripted lessons but rather through creating learning situations that promoted inquiry habits of mind throughout the school."

Some described members of the staff as 'their class'. Just as teachers had classes of students, they had classes of middle-managers and teachers. They saw themselves as responsible for teaching their class of professionals, just as the teachers were responsible for teaching their class of students. Who belonged to their class depended on the size of the school. In some larger schools, their immediate class comprised the senior managers, who then had classes of teachers. In smaller schools, the head teacher's class consisted of the teaching staff. If secondary schools had been involved, the leader of the teachers' class would most likely have been the subject department heads. Regardless of size or complexity of the school, the principal perceived their key task to be promoting inquiry habits of mind, and thus the learning of their class, in ways that ensured others within the school had the knowledge and skills to teach their class of teachers or students. Here is how one leader described the members of her class.

'Who is my class and how do I promote their learning?'

(School leader)

The principal in this school established monthly monitoring meetings for each of three grade-level teams in the school. The purpose of these meetings was to inquire into students' literacy progress in ways that could accelerate it. Towards the end of each term, the information consisted of students' progress on formal assessments administered and scored by the teachers. Other meetings were focused on what they referred to as POPs, short for 'Problems of Practice'. Each teacher brought a POP to the meeting which consisted of detailed diagnostic information about two students of concern, together with a description of the teaching approaches they had already taken to solve the students' learning problems.

When introducing the idea of these meetings, the principal talked through the purpose of the meetings with the whole staff and picked up some unease among them. She delayed the introduction of the team meetings until after a second staff meeting. She asked the teachers to bring any concerns they had. Understandably their main concerns were about being seen as less than competent if student assessments showed lower achievement than in other classes.

After talking through the concerns with the staff and assuring them of the inquiry purpose of the monitoring meetings, they went ahead with the team meetings. She attended the first meeting for each team. Two teams were engaged in lively inquiry-oriented discussions but the interactions in the third team appeared to have undercurrents of implied criticisms of some teachers. The dynamics of the situation potentially undermined learning.

An important decision for the principal was to identify who comprised her class because this determined what she should do. Having decided it was the team leaders she met with the leader of this third team and discussed the problem and its possible origins. Given the undercurrents, the main concern was to retain an inquiry focus in the meeting. They discussed how they could change the dynamics to meet this goal and the principal sat in on the next team meeting. The interactions were much improved but clearly had to be monitored. The principal and team leader followed up with another conversation in which they discussed the strategies the team leader had used and how those strategies could be shaped next time. When interviewed, the head explained the problem this way. *'We were so busy attending to the needs of the teachers in the school that we didn't attend to our leadership learning needs. This showed that I need to include the team leaders as well, in their leadership roles.'*

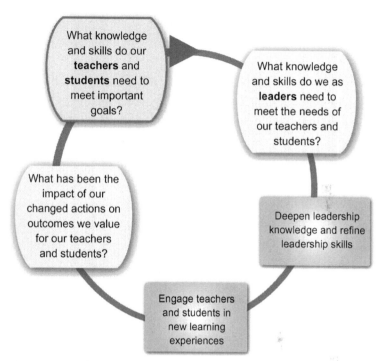

Figure 5.2 Leader inquiry and knowledge-building cycle to promote valued teaching and student outcomes

As described in this and the previous case about learning intentions, leaders as much as teachers were engaged in their own inquiry and knowledge-building cycles as illustrated in Figure 5.2. They asked themselves and each other, 'What knowledge and skills do we as leaders need to develop the relevant knowledge and skills for students and teachers?'

Relationships of respect and challenge

Relationships between leaders and teachers are central to well-functioning schools and form the platform for most other things that happen. It is not surprising that much of the research literature on leadership has the nature of those relationships at its core. One of the most important contributions to understanding how relationships contribute to school improvement comes from the research undertaken by Anthony Bryk and colleagues[65] when they studied the Chicago public school reforms in the 1980s. These authors coined the term 'relational trust'. They described how such trust is forged through day-to-day social exchanges and is defined by respect through a genuine sense of listening to others, personal regard shown by a willingness of people to extend themselves beyond what is formally required, and beliefs that colleagues have the knowledge, skills and/or technical capacity to deliver on intentions and promises.

In the participating schools, both leaders and teachers described these kinds of relationships. Teachers talked about feeling respected. They also described the challenging nature of the relationships with the leaders. They often talked about being challenged to think about student outcomes, their teaching practice and what needed to change to make the desired shifts for particular groups of students. No one shied away from evaluation of student learning or of practice and the assumptions teachers and leaders made about the connections between them. Although the essence of respect in the schools participating in the study had within it a strong sense of responsibility for student outcomes, there was no evidence of blame. Teachers talked about being challenged but never about being criticized.

These were schools in which strong opinions were held by both leaders and teachers. These opinions were discussed in ways that the reasons or the evidence underpinning them were an expected part of the conversations. As one principal explained, 'I like to be

108

as transparent as I can in my thinking.' Similarly, teachers talked about being asked to explain the reasons for their comments or statements. Through making assumptions, reasoning and evidence explicit, the leaders' and teachers' personal theories about teaching and learning became part of the debate. Comparing personal theories with more formal theories extends both teachers' and leaders' knowledge.

Part of the acceptance of these challenging conversations was the respect the leaders earned by placing themselves in learning situations. The case in the box below describes how the leader in one school did this.

'She's on the line too.'

(Teacher talking about the principal)

This school belonged to a network of schools. The network decided to focus on giving task and process feedback to students because of its central role in promoting student learning. Classroom observations had shown that teachers' feedback focused mostly on personal praise and this did not help students to reach their learning goals. Providing effective feedback to students became the network goal. Professional development was organized and the teachers wanted to know how well they were doing in reshaping their feedback practice.

The network leaders were principals. They thought about paying for extra time for the professional learning

---

provider to observe all the teachers in their classrooms but realized it would take too long given the number of teachers involved. They also realized that if they were to become leaders of learning, then maybe this was a school leadership task. There were two problems with this solution. The principals would take too long to complete the task within their schools and they did not know enough about giving feedback to either students or teachers to do it well.

They partly solved the problem by deciding that middle-level leaders in each school should undertake the classroom observations because they had attended the professional development sessions on teacher–student feedback and they could be released from other duties. This solution raised two further problems. Problem 1 – leader–teacher feedback was not the same as teacher–student feedback, so the middle leaders needed some new skills. Problem 2 – principals were removed from a learning leadership role. They decided that everyone needed to know about the principles of effective feedback and how to contextualize them for their particular situations. The teachers were learning how to give feedback to students. The middle-level leaders needed to learn how to give feedback to the teachers, and the principals to the middle-level leaders.

There was only one problem left that they could see. How would the principals know if they were giving feedback in ways that promoted professional learning? Their solution was to take turns bringing a video and transcript of a conversation they had with their mid-level leaders to the network and have other principals critique using agreed protocols. The teachers spoke in admiring terms about their leaders' preparedness to make their learning so transparent with one saying with genuine respect, *'She's on the line too.'*

In the other schools these kinds of respectful but challenging conversations also took place with teachers and parent communities, particularly in schools located in high poverty areas where teachers often held views of deficit and neglect. In three of the schools, leaders had specifically challenged their teachers to engage with the community in ways that were open to learning from them. In two of these schools, for example, teachers were required to report to parents in more open and honest ways than they had before so that parents knew exactly how their children were progressing in relation to age-related expectations. Many teachers resisted initially because they thought the parents would be angry if their children were achieving below these expectations. They were surprised when the parents showed appreciation of their honesty. Consistent with a learning framework, these reports were accompanied with suggestions about what the parents could do at home and what their teachers could use at school from home.

Integrating the domains

At the end of Chapter 4, I described the qualities of teachers when they had developed adaptive expertise. These same qualities were required of leaders if they were to know when their leadership practices were working and when they were not working and, therefore, needed to change.

The very nature of leadership, however, means that this kind of expertise must go beyond individuals and groups of teachers and apply to the school as a whole. In the organizational literature this kind of expertise is usually referred to as adaptive capacity.[66] In essence, this involves developing a school community that learns. Through some rewording, the description for individual professionals in Chapter 4 can be used as the basis for the school as an organization, because this is the responsibility of leaders. In schools developing adaptive capacity, leaders and teachers become deeply knowledgeable about both the content of what is taught and how to teach it and create the organizational structures, situations and routines to develop it further. All work to become aware of the assumptions underpinning their collective practice so they know when they are helpful and when to question them and if necessary to let them go. They become expert in retrieving, organizing and applying professional knowledge in light of the challenges presented by the students they are teaching. The routines involve being constantly vigilant about the impact of leadership and teaching on students' engagement, learning and well-being. To exercise this vigilance, they also know how to assess students and the effectiveness of teaching on what matters over both short and long time frames. They construct situations that help them to work out when known organizational routines do not work and to have sufficient knowledge to work collectively to develop innovative

> "Engaging in inquiry and knowledge-building cycles at all levels of the organization is seen as core to professionalism."

approaches when needed. Part of having adaptive capacity is to know when and from where to seek help. Engaging in inquiry and knowledge-building cycles at all levels of the organization is seen as core to their professionalism.

Reflecting on your professional learning experiences

If you are a leader, think about the last time you organized or engaged in some kind of professional learning designed to improve leadership or teaching practice or student outcomes. Together with those with whom you worked use the descriptors below to decide if your activities were at a basic, developing or integrated level. If you have not engaged in or organized professional learning, use the descriptors with your leadership team to think about how you might go about this.

Leadership of professional learning

Basic	Developing	Integrated
Professional learning is focused on teachers with leaders promoting learning and being supportive of teachers' efforts	Professional learning includes leaders taking a leadership of learning role but the learning required to undertake the role is not specifically identified or targeted	Leaders take a strong leadership role in professional learning, recognize their own need to learn how to do this and specifically seek opportunities that parallel teachers' professional learning

Building own and others' knowledge

Basic	Developing	Integrated
Leaders' pedagogical content knowledge is assumed to be adequate with no specific opportunities sought to develop it	Leaders seek opportunities to build knowledge but not necessarily pedagogical content knowledge or knowledge specific to making organizational routines around teaching and learning more effective	Leaders seek opportunities to build pedagogical content knowledge in important areas of focus with the knowledge specific to making organizational routines around teaching and learning more effective

Relationships of respect and challenge

Basic	Developing	Integrated
Relationships between leaders and teachers are respectful in the sense of being supportive but not challenging. A non-evaluative culture is encouraged	Relationships between leaders and teachers are respectful with a strong emphasis on being supportive of learning. Evaluations of student learning, teacher or leadership practice are rarely debated	Relationships between leaders and teachers are both respectful and challenging. Evaluations of student learning, teacher or leadership practice are part of the learning culture and are rigorously debated. Included in the debate are the assumptions on which those evaluations are made

If any of the activities were at a basic or developing level, decide together what each of you needs to do to move them towards becoming more integrated. What evidence might you collect to monitor if your activities are moving closer to the description at the integrated level? Decide when you will check your progress and how you will do it.

6

Bringing the Parts of the Cycle Together

So far I have looked at separate parts of the cycle and the role of leadership in promoting professional learning within schools. This chapter shifts the focus to describe two very different professional learning situations that address the whole cycle. These situations are described in extended cases that show how the dimensions can be integrated for teachers and the role leaders can take within them. The first case describes how a secondary school, embedded in a wider professional learning community, operated as a school-based learning community. The second case takes a more micro-process perspective

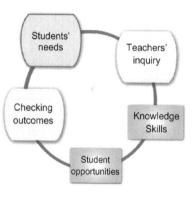

> **"**The interplay between organizational and individual expertise develops common language and understandings so important to deepening knowledge and refining skills.**"**

and identifies how coaching through the observation and analysis of teaching practice can deepen teacher learning. Both cases resulted in improved outcomes for students on challenging content.

The description of these more extended cases illustrates how the processes within them promote learning at the organizational and individual levels as the whole cycle is engaged. The interplay between organizational and individual expertise develops common language and understandings so important to deepening knowledge and refining skills.[67] How professional learning is approached within both these situations is consistent with the findings on how people learn.[68] Teachers' personal theories of teaching and learning are engaged, their knowledge is developed within conceptual frameworks, with meta-cognitive and self-regulated learning promoted.

In both these extended cases, learning opportunities have been constructed systematically, not left to chance. This does not mean that many informal exchanges and interactions both within and across schools have not contributed to professional learning; they have. It means that some of these opportunities have been deliberate and structured with time allocated. Often these more formal learning opportunities lay the groundwork for learning-focused informal interactions among teachers and leaders.

Professional learning communities

Professional learning communities go under many guises but usually refer to a group of professionals committed to working together to learn about their practice for the purpose of improving student learning.[69] Within such communities, Louise Stoll and colleagues refer to learning becoming '... a collective enterprise that ensures individual learning adds up to a coherent whole, driven by high quality pupil learning as its fundamental purpose.'[70]

Professional learning communities have a history of strong advocacy but more limited, although growing, evidence related to their effectiveness. There are parallels between professional learning communities and professional development itself. It is not simply the presence of a professional learning community or professional development that determines effectiveness, but rather what happens, the expertise that is brought to bear on the participants' deliberations, and the extent to which the processes promote learning and changes to practice in the interests of students.

Louise Stoll[71] identified seven processes for effective leadership of such communities. These include sharing a student learning focus; cultivating involvement and distributed leadership; nurturing respectful, trusting relationships; promoting collaborative enquiry that leads to deep learning; seeking evidence about professional learning community processes and outcomes; ensuring supportive structures; and drawing on external facilitators and critical friends. These processes and how they combine with the principles of how people learn are illustrated in the following extended case of a secondary school in the United Kingdom.

The context

This multicultural secondary school of 1450 students is in a mixed socio-economic area of London. The school was instrumental in the development of a borough-wide professional learning community of all secondary schools and was its 'lead school' in the first year. The aim of the community is to share learning experiences and work together to generate new knowledge and improve the culture of learning in the schools.[72] The headteacher described how thinking within the school had shifted from taking a traditional professional development focus to the school operating as a professional learning community within the borough.

> At an earlier stage as a headteacher I would have been in the place of not really believing that you could identify a clear link between professional development and student outcomes. It was quite hard to track …. In this particular approach it's really clear. Where the inception of it is at school, the whole thing remains rooted in the impact of the practice and so it never strays very far from impact. You're actually judging good practice precisely from the impact you've seen on students rather than dislocating the training from impact.

Part of the shift the headteacher described involved the restructuring of the leadership team to move from a siloed system of roles and responsibilities to making it a collective responsibility through having teaching, learning and assessment as part of all leaders' responsibilities.

The main form of inquiry across all schools in the wider professional community was a system of school reviews exploring the six personal learning and thinking skills promoted at the time within England's national secondary curriculum,[73] namely that students should be: independent inquirers, creative thinkers, reflective learners, team workers, self managers, and effective participators. Appreciative inquiry[74] was chosen as the mode of inquiry, a process of collaborative inquiry based on interviews and affirmative questioning to collect and celebrate 'good news stories' and through this identifying other areas and ways in which the school could become 'even better off'.

As with other cases described in this book, collaborative reviews and inquiries have become more focused and deeper over time. The inquiry unpacked in this extended case involves a review of the sixth form (Years 12 and 13). The problem they were trying to solve was the difficulty students experienced in moving from the more content-focused curriculum for GCSE[75] in Year 11 to developing greater independence for A levels in Years 12 and 13. The teachers were concerned that students entering Year 12 were not sufficiently prepared personally for the more challenging curriculum. The inquiry question was expressed formally as, 'How do we encourage our sixth form students to recognize and engage with the A level challenge?' A number of sub-questions followed, such as, 'How are students encouraged to be effective independent learners in and out of lessons?'

The teachers worked collaboratively to develop a set of nine indicators that were considered to be evidence of quality learning that formed the basis for deepening knowledge and refining skills within conceptual frameworks. Examples of these indicators were that students:

- provide intelligently thoughtful responses
- lead and or actively take part in student discussions
- draw considered conclusions.

The review followed the process developed across the borough in which a mixed team of 10 leaders and teachers who framed the review undertook the classroom observations and interviews, and pinpointed the successful teaching practices that showed evidence of students responding in ways that were consistent with the profile of successful learners. An overview

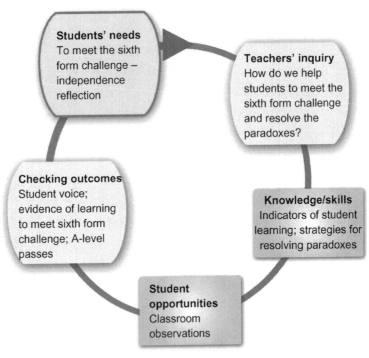

Figure 6.1 Teacher inquiry and knowledge-building cycle for sixth form review

of how the process fitted within the inquiry cycle is provided in Figure 6.1.

Identifying students' needs

In terms of external examination results, the school profiles of achievement were well above what would be expected for the mixed student population as a result of the actions taken through previous reviews. While examination results continued to be monitored, the main driver of the inquiry was the need for students in Years 12 and 13 to challenge themselves, to be more reflective and develop more independence.

An important process in identifying how students approached their learning involved the review team gathering evidence from classrooms about the circumstances under which students exhibited the quality learning indicators. The review team were paired up to observe in 16 classrooms where they recorded evidence of the indicators during the lessons. By working in pairs the reviewers deepened their own knowledge of effective practice through their discussions together and with the classroom teacher. These observations also included interviewing students using prompt questions such as, 'Can you tell me something that has really made you think in today's lesson?' Groups of students were also interviewed out of class.

The evidence from these observations was collated across classrooms by the review team for the purpose of sharing the findings with all teachers, including those who taught lower year levels. The headteacher and review team were concerned that their internal findings should be validated, so they invited an external expert to undertake a similar independent review.

Both the internal team and the external person identified a series of paradoxes in the ways students wanted to learn. For example, they wanted to be told yet they wanted to be independent. The review team summed up this particular paradox in the following statement derived from the student interviews, 'I don't like it when I don't understand [versus] if I have to struggle to understand I end up learning more.' Another statement in a similar vein comprised, 'I don't like being forced to go and find things out for myself [versus] the best homework is when you are made to think.' Rather than dismiss these paradoxes, the review team decided that they needed to learn how to structure their teaching to address them.

Identifying professional learning needs and building knowledge

As in any integrated learning situation, professional learning needs were identified and knowledge built through the process of identifying students' knowledge and skills. The development of the indicators of student learning for Years 12 and 13 meant the teachers had previously worked collaboratively to develop a common understanding of the characteristics they believed to be important for successful learning at this level. The teachers were aware that the students' approach to learning had to be different at these more advanced levels from earlier years but had difficulty describing this in anything other than general terms for themselves or their students. As one review team member explained, 'We say we want students who are independent, but what does that mean? We couldn't quite describe it'.

The classroom observations referred to above also involved gathering evidence of effective teaching practices that promoted this kind of student learning. These characteristics were not judged as effective or ineffective independently of the students' responses. As one of the review team described, 'We've stopped talking about what the teacher did and the students were a kind of by-product. ... The important question is, "How are they responding?"'

Seven members of staff who taught these levels were also interviewed with questions such as, 'How do you encourage successful independent learning?' 'How do you encourage reflection in your lessons?' These reflections engaged teachers' existing theories of practice.

The approach to the review process resulted in a seamless flow from identifying professional learning needs to building professional knowledge and promoting self-regulated learning for the review team and staff. As the headteacher explained:

> It's already drawn 10 members of staff [on the review team] into an engagement so that when we did the training day there was already a set of people who had engaged with the issue and seen the evidence and there was nothing 'done to' about it. The best practice that was observed was actually being fed into workshop sessions so the people who were caught out doing something good had a chance to talk about it.

At the beginning of the training day the staff were asked to consider two questions: What is innovative teaching in the sixth form? What is a good task in a lesson? The review team structured the day to review the qualities of learning agreed to for Years 12 and 13, and for staff to work in groups to identify the specifics of effective strategies for creating high-quality learning. Next, groups were charged with developing solutions to a specific paradox that had emerged from the review. For example, the team working on the dependence/independence paradox made several suggestions including 'Learning must not be prescriptive ... yet it must be fully scaffolded'; 'Let them be independent – but don't let them fail'. From this discussion they identified specific teaching strategies aligned with these ideas and they used follow-up sessions based in departments to continue developing and sharing effective practice to address the paradoxes.

Checking for students' learning opportunities and outcomes

This rich case was still emerging at the time of writing and so the cycle was not complete. However, they had planned ongoing checking processes. In order to check if the learning opportunities for students had changed, the school planned to continue with paired observations and teacher interviews by the review team. In addition, they intended that observations undertaken as part of the performance management system would use the same indicators and would be formally collated by heads of department to feed into the whole school self-evaluation system.

Checking whether students were coping better with the demands of Years 12 and 13 involved the inevitable ongoing analysis of the profile of A-level passes. But this was not the main focus of the review. In order to determine whether students were meeting the challenge of these higher levels of schooling more effectively, the review team planned to ask students about the resolution of the paradoxes and to observe them, using the same criteria as before. In addition, the observations that formed part of the performance management system formally contributed to information about whether students were developing the learning skills identified as relevant to meeting the learning challenge.

Bringing the case together

Achieving whole school professional learning in secondary schools is not easy. This school has developed sophisticated systems for engaging teachers in professional learning in ways that promote deep student learning. The processes for effective leadership of professional learning communities identified by Louise Stoll[76] were evident in this extended case as the leaders and teachers engaged in the cycle of inquiry and knowledge-building. The student learning focus was apparent through all phases. Leadership of the learning review was distributed across staff at all levels through involvement in the review team. Relationships were respectful and trusting as a result of the process of appreciative inquiry and the way the discussions for improvement were structured. The inquiry process was highly collaborative and led to increasingly deep learning. The review team closely monitored the process to ensure it worked for the teachers. External expertise was used to check and validate the internal processes.

Coaching through observation and analysis of practice

This second extended case is also situated within a wider community in that it describes the approach to observations and analysis of practice within the literacy project in New Zealand that I referred to in the first chapter. In this case the specifics are illustrated through a single conversation between a leader and teacher.

Coaching can refer to almost any job-embedded activity but Susan L'Allier and colleagues[77] from the United States identified that student achievement gains were greater when coaches spent time observing teaching and providing supportive feedback. I have focused on this activity in this second case.

The context

Observations and analysis of practice have been major activities in the literacy professional development project. The visiting literacy experts work with school leaders to become teacher coaches. Over time, the emphasis has shifted from the coach observing and giving supportive feedback to a teacher to more of a partnership in which both coach and teacher analyse teaching practice together. Their analysis is based on teachers' learning goals and a shared understanding about effective practice. Accompanying this shift towards a partnership has been a shift to referring to the conversations as practice analysis conversations. Teachers have consistently rated these conversations as having a very powerful influence on their professional learning.

The practice analysis conversation model emerged from several problems that were evident in coaching conversations early in the project. In these early conversations, criteria for effective practice were usually implicit rather than explicit so the teachers did not know what effective practice looked like or why it was more effective than what they were already doing. This problem was compounded when coaches made recommendations for change that focused on practical strategies with no explanation of why those strategies might be more effective than what they did before. Because students' responses to the practice of focus were rarely included in the conversation, the discussions about practice were divorced from the reactions of those it was designed to benefit.

These problems were addressed by establishing protocols for the conversations. The protocols are in three parts, involving a pre-observation conversation, the observation itself, and a practice analysis conversation following the observation. The conversations

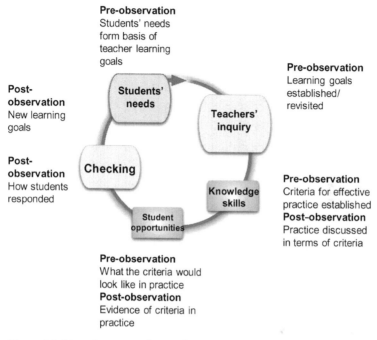

Figure 6.2 How the pre- and post-observation conversations fit into the knowledge-building cycle

are designed to engage teachers' personal theories of practice, build deep knowledge within conceptual frameworks, and develop meta-cognitive and self-regulated learning.[78] The positioning of the pre- and post-observation conversations in relation to the inquiry and knowledge-building cycle is shown in Figure 6.2. The protocols for the conversations are illustrated with an edited conversation with a teacher relatively new to the profession that was recorded and analysed as part of the project research.[79] This conversation has been selected to describe a teacher that coaches throughout the world are likely to recognize, rather than one who was highly expert.

The pre-observation conversation

Teachers' learning goals are at the centre of the pre-observation conversation because goals are fundamental to developing meta-cognition and self-regulated learning. They provide the teacher with direction and the basis for judging their professional progress. Teachers' learning goals are first and foremost based on students' needs and are focused on an area of priority which is likely to assist students to make better sense of something they need to learn in order to make progress. In this way, the teachers' learning goals link the first two dimensions of the cycle of student and teacher learning.

Teachers' beliefs are engaged through the teacher and coach jointly developing criteria for effectiveness with respect to the practice of focus and discussing why those criteria are important. Just as students need to know what success looks like and why, so do teachers. It is important that the criteria are co-constructed in ways that unpack each other's meaning. The teacher explains his or her understandings and the coach helps the teacher to probe these understandings and also contributes their expert knowledge. The process can be made more robust if they draw on wider expert knowledge when constructing these criteria. In the transcript below, for example, the teacher was trying to help the six-year-old students make connections between what they were reading about catching rabbits and their real world experiences. In order to establish these criteria, the coach said to the teacher, 'We need to revisit what it means to make connections and why this is

> "Teachers' beliefs are engaged through the teacher and coach jointly developing criteria for effectiveness with respect to the practice of focus and discussing why those criteria are important."

important' and referred to a handbook on effective literacy practice to help them.

Knowledge is deepened during the next step of deciding together what the criteria for effectiveness would look like in practice. Discussing the specifics of practice within the criteria deepens understanding about what the criteria really mean. In the transcript below, the coach asks, 'When I come to observe, how will I know what to look for when you are helping the students to make connections and how will I know they have got it?'

Most coaching relationships involve a variety of interactions between teachers and coaches, such as workshops, as well as the analysis of practice. If concepts relevant to the practice of focus have been discussed in these other situations, they should be incorporated into the pre-observation conversation so the analysis of practice is situated within a wider professional learning framework.

I have referred to the importance of developing relationships of trust and challenge several times because of their fundamental importance in any professional learning relationship. Trust and challenge also underpin an effective coaching relationship. Having one's practice observed and analysed is high stakes and it is important to understand that personal anxieties are likely to arise, particularly in the early stages. Jointly establishing the focus, being open about the criteria and ensuring that their meanings are shared, builds trust. Once this kind of coaching becomes part of the routines of professional learning, teachers actively seek opportunities to help solve ongoing problems of practice. In this conversation, the coach is the curriculum leader. It begins after preliminary greetings.

COACH: 'So let's revisit the learning goal you established last time. Looking at our notes here, we noticed that some of the slower progress students were not making connections between their reading and what they already knew. At this early stage of their reading, they were focused on the text and not using their real world experiences. You wanted to work out how you could help them to make connections in ways that would lead to them to do this independently.'

TEACHER: 'Yes, I've done quite a lot of work on this. I think I'm getting better and they're getting better.'

COACH: 'Ok, we need to revisit what we both mean by making connections and how this might help the students with their reading just to make sure we are on the same page.'

[Conversation establishes shared understandings. They checked the criteria they developed by referring to a handbook on effective literacy practice.]

COACH: 'So let's focus specifically on this lesson. When I come to observe, how will I know what to look for when you are helping the students to make connections and how will I know they have got it? What book are you reading with the students and what connections do you want them to make?'

[Conversation continues with specifics of the lesson and a decision made that both would pay attention to the prompts the teacher was using to help the students to make connections. Organizational arrangements were finalized.]

The observation

Careful notes need to be taken during the observation to ensure an accurate record is available for the next part of the conversation. It is also important to find out how students are responding to what the teacher does because their responses form the basis of ongoing professional learning goals. There are many ways to find this out including asking students about their understanding of the lesson, observing the students' discussions during the lesson, or examining their work. The coach in this case took careful note of the prompts the teacher was using and other interactions with the students in the reading group. Notes related to connections included questions such as, 'Have you ever held a rabbit?' with the students' responses recorded. Notes not directly related to making connections included a question when one student was stuck on an unknown word, 'Do you know a word that starts the same but ends in "ing"?'

The analysis of practice

The main focus of this part of the conversation remains with the teacher's goals and the indicators of progress the teacher is making towards achieving those goals. The reference points are the criteria worked out in the pre-observation conversation together with the evidence in that particular lesson. If other things get in the way of achieving this goal, then they too need to be raised. Keeping the focus on professional goals develops the meta-cognitive and self-regulated learning that is the long-term aim of such coaching interactions. Teachers who can continue to set and monitor learning goals in the absence of the coach are those who will continue to improve their practice and become adaptive experts.

Through discussing the criteria, their evidence in practice, and the students' responses, knowledge is deepened within a conceptual framework of effective practice. Disagreements about the evidence and what it means are resolved by reference to the theory on which the criteria are based and how the students responded. These points in the conversations are challenging for coaches. They must be able to draw on a deep theoretical knowledge base to explain to a teacher why one particular practice might be more effective than another and why students are more likely to benefit from it.

The process of deepening knowledge also involves probing teachers' existing beliefs about practice so the coach understands why the teacher chose particular practices within the lesson. The complexity of teaching and learning environments means that practice is never 'pure'. When teachers try to teach in ways consistent with the agreed criteria, they are also concerned about other things, including maintaining student engagement and achieving broader lesson goals. Rather than a coach having a mindset of, 'This was effective or ineffective', the mindset must be one of inquiry, such as, 'I wonder what led the teacher to do this or that?' A question a coach might ask a teacher could be, 'Can you take me through the details, and what was going on for you because I need to understand that if I'm going to help you sort this one out.'

> **"**The process of deepening knowledge also involves probing teachers' existing beliefs about practice so the coach understands why the teacher chose particular practices within the lesson.**"**

Through these kinds of conversations teachers move around the dimensions of the inquiry and knowledge-building cycle, deepening knowledge and refining skills, engaging students in new learning experiences and checking how students respond. A continuation of the conversation above illustrates some of these points. During the conversation, it became apparent that the teacher did not understand what the goals they had discussed really meant in practice.

COACH: 'Ok, let's just review where we got to. This group of students weren't making connections between what they were reading and their prior experience and you wanted them to learn to do this independently. You wanted us both to notice the prompts you used to help them make connections to the text.'

TEACHER: 'I felt I was doing a lot of prompting and referring back to my learning objective. Sione understood better than the girls. He made really good connections to when he caught a rabbit.'

COACH: 'Yes I agree with you. When you introduced the text you used a lot of prompts. I think Sione made much better connections than the girls both during the discussion and during the reading. Let's look at what was happening for each of them. How about we start with Sione.'

[Coach and teacher examine the record of prompts the teacher used at the beginning of the lesson together with the students' responses. They concluded that Sione was able to make the connections because he had an experience of catching rabbits at home. Catching rabbits was not something the girls had experienced, so they did not respond to the prompts during the discussion and struggled with the reading.]

COACH: 'So one thing we can take from this is that for children of this age, helping them to make connections to what they are reading means they need something to hang the reading and the discussion onto. For Sione he was able to use his prior experience to respond to the prompts and then to work out the unknown words in the text. But for the girls their lack of prior experience meant that they struggled with both.'

TEACHER: 'I felt the girls had the gist of what they needed to do. They sounded out the words well and they thought the rabbit was clever.'

COACH: 'That fits with what I observed, because most of the time you were working with the girls on sounding out words rather than making connections. I was wondering what led you to do that.'

[Teacher explains that the text was difficult for them with so many unknown words. She believed that they had to work out the unknown words before she could move onto helping them make connections to real world experiences.]

COACH: 'So what was happening for the girls was the text was difficult and they didn't have any prior experience to make connections to help them to understand it. That made the task very difficult for them.'

TEACHER: 'Yes I guess so.'

COACH: 'So it seems to me part of the challenge for you is to identify the texts that are right for particular learning aims. Would you like me to help you develop some criteria for choosing texts that are best to use. The sort of thing I'm thinking of is listing some of the strategies we've been talking about to help students understand what they are reading. Then listing the kinds of texts that will help them to do that – the content they have, the difficulty level for the students and so on. And maybe some key prompts for you and what you need to look for.'

[They decide that developing such a list would be useful for all the teachers of junior reading and to make it a priority to discuss this at their next team meeting.]

After establishing how teachers can improve the specifics of the practice of focus, the cycle is completed by the coach and teacher discussing how the teacher can monitor whether his or her new practice is more effective for the students than before. In the situation of this transcript, this discussion occurred after the team meeting. The teacher's next learning goal involved selecting appropriate texts and prompting for specific lesson aims. In this way another cycle of inquiry and knowledge-building was engaged.

Bringing the case together

One-on-one coaching interactions are expensive in terms of professional learning time. The objective must be to use this time in ways that challenge and develop teachers' deep understanding of practice and develop adaptive expertise. Then teachers are able to select appropriate strategies for those teachable moments that arise unpredictably in students' learning environments and on a more long-term basis. Leaders work to develop the adaptive capacity of the school as a whole. In this way both leaders and teachers intentionally reflect on routines of practice and think about when they do and do not work. They develop sufficient knowledge to take different approaches when they need to. The early career teacher in the above conversation had a long way to go. Through the interactions with her coach and her colleagues, she gradually developed an inquiry habit of mind that focused her on becoming responsive to her students and thinking of effectiveness in terms of what she was doing to promote their learning in very specific ways.

Bringing the two cases together

These two extended cases illustrate how the whole cycle of inquiry and knowledge-building can be engaged over an extended period or in just one conversation. What was common to both cases was that professional learning was embedded in the daily routines of both schools. Although it looked very different in the two schools, the underlying processes were consistent with the findings on how people learn.

They were also consistent with the qualities of evidence-informed conversations identified in the diagram in Figure 2.1. Relationships of respect and challenge pervaded the interactions. Through using relevant evidence and accessing expert knowledge the teachers and their leaders consistently demonstrated inquiry habits of mind in the interests of their students. Improved outcomes for the students were the result.

Reflecting on your professional learning experiences

Think about the routines you have within your school for engaging leaders and teachers in professional learning. Together with those with whom you worked, use the descriptors below to decide if your activities were at a basic, developing or integrated level. What evidence do you have to support your decision? Do others have evidence that leads to a different decision?

The integration of professional learning

Basic	Developing	Integrated
Professional learning is separate from most other school processes	Professional learning involves the whole school but problems of teaching and learning are not explicitly shared	Professional learning is part of a whole school challenge to solve agreed problems of teaching and learning and integrated into the school's routines

Criteria for effective practice

Basic	Developing	Integrated
Criteria for effective practice are assumed rather than made explicit and debated	Criteria for effective practice are made explicit by leaders but their worth is assumed rather than being debated by the whole staff	Criteria for effective practice are explicit and debated as an integral part of professional learning whatever form it takes

Engaging in the whole cycle

Basic	Developing	Integrated
Few aspects of the cycle are evident in school-based professional learning. Most emphasis is on building teacher knowledge and practice	Most aspects of the cycle are evident in school-based professional learning but some are not an explicit part, such as checking for improved student outcomes in the area of focus	All aspects of the cycle are evident in school-based professional learning and form an integral part of the school's approach. Similar processes are evident if the school networks with other schools

If any of the activities were at a basic or developing level, decide together what each of you needs to do to move them towards becoming more integrated. What evidence might you collect to monitor if your activities are moving closer to the description at the integrated level? Decide when you will check your progress and how you will do it.

7

Some Challenges in Facilitating Professional Learning

The approach to professional learning I have described in this book has implications for those who facilitate this learning. In the previous two chapters I have described situations where in-school leaders have led professional learning for their teachers. There are many situations,

however, where it is appropriate to involve someone external to the school to build the professional capabilities of leaders and/or teachers within schools. Many of the cases described in this book have involved external facilitation. This is a challenging role.

I have referred to these external people as professional learning facilitators rather than professional development providers because their primary role is to work in partnership with leaders and teachers to build their capabilities so they are able to take control of their own learning in the future in the interests of students. In different countries people who provide these kinds of service are located in different places. They may be part of the formal system of provincial, district or local authority offices, or heads of neighbouring schools; part of higher education systems such as universities or colleges of education; or independent of either of these groups. Although I have focused on the facilitation of learning by those external to the school in this chapter, the issues I discuss are also relevant to those in-school leaders with responsibility for professional learning.

> "Professional learning in this book focuses on involving all teachers developing professional and organizational adaptive expertise in which the reflective skills bring together evidence about outcomes for students together with teaching and leadership practice."

The location of professional learning facilitators is not as important as the theory of professionalism underpinning their work and the extent to which their practices are consistent with this theory. In Chapter 1, I referred to Walter Doyle's portrayal of teachers as professionals. One portrayal was of the good employee who maintained the prevailing norms of school practices. Within this framework, the approach to promoting learning is to show teachers how to do it right through a range of activities designed to enhance their understanding. Professional development providers who begin their interactions with teachers at the point in the inquiry and knowledge-building cycle of 'Deepening knowledge and refining skills' are usually operating from good employee assumptions of professionalism. I referred earlier to the undercurrents that can arise when professional learning providers believe that teachers have major improvements to make to their practice, while teachers attending their sessions think that little needs to change.[80]

Walter Doyle contrasts this notion of professionalism with the reflective professional able to draw on an integrated knowledge base to improve practice through reflection and inquiry. Approaches to professional learning that encourage teachers to choose from a range of courses or to develop within-school study groups are usually based on this notion of professionalism. While this kind of experience may help to deepen teachers' professional knowledge there is little evidence that substantive change in outcomes for students is likely unless it is associated with a specific teaching or learning problem to solve. The other limitation of this approach is that those who choose to participate are often those who are already effective. The question becomes 'What do we do with the others?' A system lift requires more than the willing to be involved.

The view of professionalism developed throughout this book is about the kinds of reflective practice by teachers and leaders that have an impact on all students, particularly those who are not doing as well as others in our education systems. Its focus is on involving all teachers developing adaptive expertise in which their reflective skills bring together evidence about outcomes for students together with teaching and leadership practice to look for relationships among them. It also develops inquiry habits of mind that lead to interrogating this evidence in ways that challenge existing assumptions about how to be effective. It builds professional knowledge and skills to solve the problems identified through the inquiry process. Although this portrayal may appear to be an unrealistic ideal, the ideal has become reality in a wide range of schools and situations described in ordinary classrooms and ordinary schools in the cases throughout this book. The difference they have made to outcomes for students has been extraordinary.

Creating the need to know

Facilitators of professional learning have a more challenging role than those based on apprenticeship or reflective professional models of learning. The primary role of the facilitator is to develop leaders' and teachers' capabilities to move around the inquiry and knowledge-building cycle by creating the need to know how to analyse in detail the specific problems of learning, teaching and leading, developing the capabilities to solve them and checking if they have done so. The show, tell and practice activities within the apprenticeship model may be appropriate at some points in the process provided they are motivated by the participants' need to know. Activities consistent with the reflective view of professionalism are also employed but they are accompanied by an appropriate evidence base focused on students and teaching within a context of the need to know.

Meeting this facilitation challenge is easier if new ideas are similar to those already held by participating leaders and teachers than if they create dissonance with current beliefs about curriculum content, students and/or the kinds of relationships with them that are considered appropriate. For this reason, I have focused on the issue of creating and resolving dissonance in this section. By dissonance I mean the extent to which new ideas and existing ideas might be in conflict with one another. For example, if teachers have previously taught science as a set of facts to be learned by students, and then are asked to teach science using inquiry-based approaches, they are likely to experience some level of conflict or dissonance between their current beliefs and the new ideas presented. Earlier I referred to the problem of over-assimilation[81] when teachers believe that they understand new ideas but do so

at a superficial level only. This problem is particularly evident in
situations in which teachers experience dissonance as they try to
resolve conflicting ideas within their existing cognitive frameworks.
In the science example, over-assimilation would be evident if the
teachers then tried to teach the same set of facts using inquiry-based
approaches rather than rethinking what it means to engage with an
inquiry-based curriculum.

An area in which it is possibly most difficult to create and resolve dissonance in ways that lead to new relationships and practice
involves racism in teaching. Russell Bishop[82] has spent many years
in a research and development role addressing this issue in New
Zealand secondary schools for Māori students, New Zealand's in-
digenous population, in a project called 'Te Kōtahitanga'. Māori students as a group have a more negative experience of New Zealand
schooling than students from the majority groups. This experience is
reflected in achievement and attendance statistics. Following teachers' participation in the project, indicators of Māori engagement
in school and academic achievement improved significantly. His
approach to creating and resolving dissonance for teachers in the
early stages of the project is described in the case below.

'She doesn't even congratulate you if you've done something
good. She doesn't smile either.'

(Māori student talking about his teacher)

Te Kōtahitanga is focused on reducing disparities in
educational outcomes for Māori students by helping
teachers to reflect critically on the assumptions they make

about their relationships and interactions with them. The teachers begin their participation at a three-day meeting located in a traditional Māori setting in which appropriate cultural protocols are followed. Early on in the meeting the teachers are presented with stories from engaged and non-engaged students, their parents and a selection of teachers and principals compiled from earlier research. The stories show that each of these groups have markedly different perceptions of what it is like to be a Māori student in a New Zealand classroom. The most divergent views are the ones expressed by the teachers and the students.

The teachers attributed the difficulties experienced by Māori students to deficiencies in the students themselves and their backgrounds. They believed that Māori learners were simply less capable of high educational achievement because of limited language skills and poor home backgrounds. From their perspective, these factors were the underlying causes of students' low achievement, high absenteeism and disruptive behaviour.

In contrast, the students' own stories focused primarily on their classroom experiences and their relationships and interactions with teachers. They spoke about the negative attitudes and beliefs they experienced and their feelings of being excluded. They also identified positive relationships with some teachers where the teachers knew and trusted them and made an effort to know them as Māori. Further, they described how they believed their achievement could be enhanced if their teachers would use teaching approaches that were more inclusive than the expert–novice transmission model they most often experienced.

These contrasting stories served to create dissonance for the teachers. The ways in which this dissonance was engaged and resolved drew upon wider Māori cultural understandings, along with those of the students. Teacher learning experiences mirrored those they were being asked to use with their Māori students. Rather than telling teachers what changes they should make, opportunities were provided for them to engage in discussion about issues that they themselves had identified from these stories. In this way they were able to formulate their learning needs as mutually agreed goals based on a different perception of their Māori students.

Having created the need for the teachers to know how to engage their Māori students differently, the professional learning facilitators then helped the teachers to construct profiles of teaching approaches more consistent with those the students had articulated. The three-day meeting was followed with intensive in-class support once the teachers returned to school.

The voice of the student in the heading for this case was replaced by another who said, 'You can tell he respects us because when it comes to learning big time he's always there.'

Smart tools for creating the need to know

In any professional learning situation, whether the ideas promoted are similar to teachers' existing beliefs about teaching and learning, or dissonant with them, personal interactions are usually complemented with material resources that I referred to in Chapter 5 as 'smart tools'.[83] Smart tools convey particular ideas involved in a task and are constructed in ways that allow the learner to engage with those ideas. The students' and teachers' stories in the case above constituted smart tools that complemented the personal interactions between facilitators and teachers. The task involved developing the teachers' need to know how to relate differently to Māori students. Further research on smart tools[84] showed that those most effective in promoting professional learning required the users to locate their practice in some way in relation to the ideas conveyed by the tool which also provided a vision about how to move forward. The teachers' collaborative discussions about their practice in relation to Māori students formed this first function of locating their current practice. The profiles of teaching approaches developed with the guidance of the facilitators formed the second function of providing a direction for improvement.

Smart tools can be particularly useful when professional learning facilitators are working with school leaders to become leaders of learning within their schools. The tools can help to convey important ideas through system layers. Any tool, like the students' stories, is usually accompanied by particular routines around their use for the process to be effective. These routines require particular attention when developing facilitation capability in others. It is not difficult to see how the collaborative stories of students and teachers could be used in less constructive ways than described in the case above.

This issue of effective and ineffective routines is further developed in the next section.

The facilitator's class

In the chapter on leadership, I promoted the idea that within-school leaders have a class of teachers who, in turn, have a class of students. The class of a facilitator of professional learning comprises those they are working with in schools. If a facilitator is a school head providing systems support to a number of schools, then it is likely that the class will comprise the leadership teams in these other schools. It may also include some of the teachers. Whatever the designation of the class, it is likely to have diverse learning needs, just as students in teachers' classes have diverse learning needs. The job of the facilitator is to work in partnership with the members of the class to identify and address those needs in the interests of students. Working in partnership means being open about processes and their purposes; the reasons for collecting evidence; and jointly interpreting its meaning. This process is sometimes referred to as 'working with' rather than 'doing to' teachers. This facilitation role is likely to be different from traditional professional development roles and creates new facilitation challenges resulting in facilitators needing to engage in inquiry and knowledge-building cycles for themselves in order to engage their class. This idea is represented in the small diagram at the beginning of this chapter.

The specific needs of the members of the facilitator's class will vary according to the outcomes that the participants have prioritized for their students. These needs will determine what the facilitator needs to learn and do to promote the learning of his or her class. To do this they need both specific knowledge of the focus area (e.g. teaching mathematics, developing student relationships) and knowledge and skills of facilitation (e.g. how to create the need to know). The following case describes the reflections of an experienced facilitator with deep knowledge of literacy, but less knowledge of the facilitation of professional learning in the early stages of her work with schools. She quickly found that she needed to learn how to integrate both these areas. Her literacy knowledge alone was not enough to engage her class in identifying their professional learning needs through the use of a hypothetical scenario of teaching practice. The case also illustrates the need to engage in appropriate routines around particular tools in order for their purpose to be clear. The routines can determine whether they become smart tools or ones that potentially undermine learning.

'It was a shock to everyone concerned.'[85]

(Visiting facilitator to schools)

Early in the facilitator's contact with schools, leaders and teachers were asked to respond to a hypothetical scenario of teaching practice that was designed to help them identify their professional learning needs. The scenario described a lesson in which the learning goals for the students were misaligned with the lesson activities that were, in turn, misaligned with the assessment task. Superficially, the lesson activities were those generally accepted as effective, but reading the scenario as a whole revealed the misalignment. The teachers were asked to rate various aspects of the lesson and to write two pieces of feedback they would give to the work of a student. Once the scenario was completed by individuals, their ratings and the reasons for them were supposed to be discussed in groups. Why were their ratings so diverse? What did this tell them about what they needed to learn? They were supposed to use this information, together with assessment information on students' literacy profiles, interviews and observations completed a few days earlier, to develop the focus for their professional learning. The facilitator explained her initial problems in working with teachers using the scenario.

> It was really difficult for me. It was much easier for me to launch in with my literacy pack and tell them how to teach reading. Instead we began with finding out about teacher knowledge using the scenario. At this stage, I didn't really know why I was doing this and I didn't explain it to the teachers. The evidence about teacher knowledge in one school showed us that whilst they had committed teachers they didn't have strong pedagogical content knowledge relating to teaching reading. That created angst for us and I wasn't sure how to handle it. Then using the scenario to present that back to teachers who had strong beliefs about how to teach literacy even though they didn't have much knowledge – it really created a hornet's nest.

> In this school, there had been a culture of positivity among staff. They [the leaders and teachers] didn't think they had much to learn. It was a shock to everybody concerned. And when I came in with, 'I expect you to self-reflect about your practice', that was met with huge resistance. The student data actually showed that the children were performing way below the mean.

She went on to describe how she sought the assistance of the project leader to work through a process closer to one of an open partnership that resulted in teachers shifting from being resistant about having their professional practice questioned to becoming engaged in the process. The facilitator recognized that part of her problem was that her limited understanding of the purpose of the scenario at this early stage had led to an exercise in gathering evidence *about* them rather than *with* them. The next time she used the scenario with a group of teachers she explained the purpose more clearly and went through the process more slowly, with a much more positive reaction.

Facilitator skills and tasks

As noted in the case above, facilitating the professional learning of one's class requires skills of facilitation as well as specific knowledge in the area of focus. As in any teaching situation, these skills form a complex combination requiring flexibility in their use depending on the needs of a particular professional class at a given time. Facilitators in the literacy professional development project who were experienced in using the inquiry and knowledge-building cycle identified collectively the knowledge and skills they believed they needed to facilitate professional learning in schools in which they worked. I have listed the tasks they identified below.[86]

Identifying students' learning needs

- Assist teachers to:
    - use evidence to investigate what students know and need to learn.

Identifying teachers' learning needs

- Assist teachers to:
    - use evidence to judge current teaching practice
    - unpack links between personal theories and current teaching practices
    - close gaps between teaching and student learning
    - relate the specifics of practice to conceptual frameworks
    - co-construct a plan to address teachers' learning needs
    - link sites of learning to deepen knowledge and to aid transfer to different contexts
    - understand purpose and rationale of facilitator actions.

Identifying leaders' learning needs

- Scaffold leaders to set up processes to support teacher learning.

- Co-construct a plan to address leaders' learning needs by identifying their responsibilities to lead the learning in their schools.

Checking effectiveness

- Assist teachers and leaders to use evidence:
  - of teaching practice to understand changes for students;
  - of student learning to monitor progress;
  - of both the above to guide decisions about future actions.

The specifics of any such list will differ according to the situation. For example, the priorities for student learning within this project were already established. Where these priorities are not so clear, a major task might be to assist leaders and teachers to identify outcomes for students that will form the focus of professional learning.

Having established the list of tasks above, the facilitators rated them according to the difficulty they experienced in enacting them. Tasks considered relatively easy involved the use of evidence to establish student learning needs, teaching practice and monitoring progress. Tasks rated as most difficult were the two that focused on leaders. Co-constructing a plan to meet leaders' learning needs was much more challenging than working with teachers to co-construct a plan to address their needs. No doubt some of the leaders involved were not expecting to have their learning needs incorporated into the development plan. These leaders experienced considerable dissonance making the shift from perceiving professional development as being about teachers to understanding that it meant new kinds of leadership knowledge and practice. Teacher-related items that were rated as relatively difficult involved theory: unpacking the links between personal theories and practice and relating the specifics of practice to conceptual frameworks.

What becomes important in identifying these kinds of tasks is the support facilitators need to learn how to enact the range of facilitation tasks in any professional learning situation – particularly those they find most difficult. Just like students, teachers and leaders require extended learning opportunities to learn new ways of working. Expecting facilitators to work differently from traditional delivery models does not mean they know how.

Addressing resistance

I have provided the challenge throughout this book that professional learning should be focused on making a difference for all students, particularly those who are least engaged in our current education system. By implication, this means that professional learning should involve all teachers. The challenge for facilitators is that not all teachers are motivated to learn. One way often used to overcome this motivation problem is to work with volunteers even though it means some teachers are missed.

A surprising finding from the best evidence synthesis on professional learning and development was that outcomes for students were no better or worse if teachers volunteered or faced pressure to participate. So working with volunteers does not necessarily work either. This finding was explained through examining

> "Teachers, who believe their personal theories about effectiveness have at best been overlooked, or at worst denigrated, are likely to become resistant."

the evidence more closely to find that some volunteers did not expect to change their practice in any substantive way and became less enthusiastic when faced with such an expectation. Some of those who faced pressure to participate became engaged when they found that the focus was on solving the problems they were experiencing with the engagement, learning and/or well-being of their students. By focusing on evidence about students in their class and the challenges they presented, the need to find out how to meet identified challenges became the motivating force. The professional learning opportunities were perceived as immediately relevant to their teaching situation. Through this evidence-informed process, initial resistance mostly disappeared. Teacher engagement at some point in the process was the important factor, not volunteering.

Competing theories

If, as commonly happens, the introduction to a particular professional learning focus begins with new approaches to teaching and learning rather than analysing students' needs, resistance is more likely to arise because competition between theories of practice[87] immediately becomes an issue for many of those participating. In this situation, competition between theories means that what individual teachers value and how they construct their practice in relation to those values are not the same as the values and practice being promoted by the professional learning facilitator. The example I described about teaching science as facts or as an inquiry process earlier in this chapter is an example of competing theories of practice. When a professional learning facilitator introduces theories that are in competition with those of the teachers the issue can become one of whose theory is better. The question that needed to be addressed to resolve competing theories in the science example is how students will benefit from engaging in an inquiry process rather than memorizing scientific facts. I raised the importance of engaging theories of practice in Chapter 1 in relation to the first of Bransford and colleagues'[88] findings about how people learn. Engaging theories of practice is about identifying and resolving competing theories.

These competing theories may extend beyond particular practices to include the essence of what it means for a teacher to be expert. In these situations expectations of change can impinge on a teacher's professional identity with more than just changing practice at stake. Personal theories of practice develop over time and for experienced teachers these theories will have developed over years, often without ever being challenged. Because the practices based on these theories have worked for the particular teacher (if not they would have been revised) they are assumed to be effective. The idea that expertise comes from experience is promoted in stage theories of professional development.[89] Most of these theories propose a general pattern of an initial phase of survival and rule-following; one or more intermediate stages of greater flexibility, experimentation and consolidation; and a final phase of mastery and fluency. By this final stage, the novice's rule-following has been transformed into skilful know-how in which problems are identified intuitively and holistically with appropriate strategies enacted to solve them. Many experienced teachers assume

> **"**Engaging theories and not dismissing them through using relevant evidence, showing an inquiry habit of mind within relationships of respect and challenge are central to resolving difference in ways that lead to mutual learning and change.**"**

they have reached this final stage of fluency. To then be told that new approaches to teaching and relationships with students should be adopted not only challenges their theories about how to teach but also challenges teachers' professional identity of being experts.

The practice-makes-perfect assumptions underpinning stage theories of professional development can divert attention from scrutinizing the worth of particular practices for promoting outcomes for students. Jian Wang and Sandra Odell,[90] for example, identified that images of teaching effectiveness held by novices and more experienced teachers in the United States had strong similarities. The accumulation of teaching experiences does not automatically change general orientations towards teaching and what is involved in teachers' work. Some of the enduring beliefs and practices they identified are likely to be problematic in a rapidly changing twenty-first-century world where knowledge is being redefined in unexpected ways, as are ideas about how best to acquire it, by an increasingly diverse student body. In primary schools, for example, both novices and experts saw teaching to be primarily about the transmission of subject matter from teacher to student. Teachers demonstrate knowledge and skills for students, followed by student practice. Ideas about student diversity remained narrow and underdeveloped regardless of experience.

Thus asking teachers to change may evoke competing theories about practice that, in turn, impinge on professional identities. I turn once again to the model of evidence-informed conversations presented in Figure 2.1 to draw out some principles about engaging competing theories in ways that are more likely to lead to their resolution. Relevant evidence is the first component. In this situation, such evidence includes teachers' current theories of practice, what they consider to be effective and how they feel about having their theories challenged. What do they disagree with? What do they agree with?

The second component, having an inquiry habit of mind, applies as much to facilitators as it does to teachers. Framing resistance as competing theories is more likely to lead to inquiry habits of mind than framing resistance as not wanting to change. What theories underpin teachers' reluctance to change? Inquiry habits of mind are closely related to the third dimension of relationships of respect and challenge. Together these two dimensions demand that teachers' existing theories are taken seriously. The facilitators' questions become, therefore, 'What leads this particular teacher to hold this particular theory? On what is it based? What are its merits? What are the limitations?' The final arbiter of merits and limitations is how competing theories and the evidence underpinning them impact on student engagement, learning and well-being. These questions become matters for debate through which facilitators also learn. In the best evidence synthesis on professional learning and development, some studies documented changes in teaching practice in line with the facilitators' recommendations but no change in student outcomes resulted.[91] Facilitators of professional learning do not always get it right.

The fourth component, accessing expertise, may contribute to resolving competing theories if the teachers perceive the expertise to be relevant. If not, then the task is to develop ways to assess the worth of the different theories and the evidence on which the expertise is based. In the case above in which the leaders and teachers believed their literacy teaching to be adequate, and therefore did not have much to learn, the students' achievement was low. Under these circumstances comparisons with schools with similar student populations but using teaching approaches based on different theories can be powerful. In the Te Kōtahitanga project, teachers' and students' competing theories about Māori student engagement and achievement were used as the catalyst for change. Engaging theories and not dismissing them through using relevant evidence, showing an inquiry habit of mind within relationships of respect and challenge are central to resolving difference in ways that lead to mutual learning and change.

The challenging role of facilitation

I have described the primary role of facilitators of professional learning as one involving a partnership with leaders and teachers to work through cycles of inquiry and knowledge-building in ways that build adaptive expertise so they can take control of their own learning in the future. The purpose of the activity is to improve outcomes for students. In this chapter I have focused on some enduring challenges faced by most facilitators in this role.

In concluding this chapter, I wish to highlight briefly one area I have mentioned in passing but not yet emphasized. This is the area of specialist expertise in the area of focus. Our research knowledge of approaches to teaching specific curriculum content, cross-curricular pedagogical approaches and the kinds of teacher–student relationships that make a difference has grown exponentially in the last decade. Facilitators of professional learning need to be cognisant of this knowledge in their area of expertise so that they can make it available and relevant to school leaders and teachers. Developing this knowledge is yet another challenge of facilitation.

Helping teachers and leaders to develop this knowledge in ways that they understand it deeply so that they can draw on it in the moment-to-moment decisions they make every day in response to their students, brings together the skills of facilitation and expert knowledge in the area of focus. How this process is undertaken can be effective in promoting leaders' and teachers' adaptive expertise or not. Perhaps the most important issue for those who facilitate professional learning, therefore, is to be explicit about the theory of professionalism underpinning their work. Few would argue with the desirability of teachers having high levels of adaptive expertise working in schools with adaptive capacity where ongoing investigations into which students are benefiting and which are not lead to informed adjustments to practice. Not all professional learning approaches are consistent with this kind of professionalism. The cycle at the beginning of this chapter assumes that facilitators, along with others in the system, engage in ongoing cycles of inquiry and knowledge-building if they are to learn how to do this.

Reflecting on your professional learning experiences

Think about the last time you facilitated some kind of professional learning for school leaders or teachers. Together with those with whom you worked, decide if your activities were at a basic, developing or integrated level using the descriptors below. What evidence do you have to support your decision? Do others have evidence that leads to a different decision?

If you were a member of the group whose learning was being promoted, think about how your learning was facilitated. Was it at a basic, developing or integrated level? What evidence do you have to support your decision?

Creating the need to know

Basic	Developing	Integrated
Professional learning approach began at the point in the cycle of deepening professional knowledge and refining skills. The desire for facilitators 'to tell' is more evident than the leaders' and teachers' 'need to know'	Analysis of students' and professional learning needs undertaken but new knowledge and skills arose primarily from the facilitator's 'desire to tell' rather than the leaders' and teachers' need 'to know'	Systematic analysis of students' and professional learning needs are undertaken in partnership with teachers. The facilitator's approach flows from the leaders' and teachers' 'need to know'

Vision of professionalism

Basic	Developing	Integrated
Vision of professionalism not made explicit. Implicit approach underpinned by assumptions of the good employee	Vision of professionalism not made explicit. Implicit approach fostered knowledge of theory and practice but not of adaptive expertise	Explicit vision of professionalism based on key concepts of adaptive expertise and promoting adaptive organizational capacity

Coping with resistance

Basic	Developing	Integrated
Possible teacher resistance to new ideas remained below the surface and was implicitly treated as a problem with teacher attitudes and beliefs	Conversations engaged some teacher beliefs but differences were taken as evidence of resistance, not as competing theories in need of resolution	Conversations were carefully crafted to make explicit the differences between existing theories and new theories with disagreements treated as competing theories in need of resolution

If any of the activities were at a basic or developing level, decide together what each of you needs to do to move them towards becoming more integrated. What evidence might you collect to monitor if your activities are moving closer to the description at the integrated level? Decide when you will check your progress and how will you do it.

8

Keeping It All Going

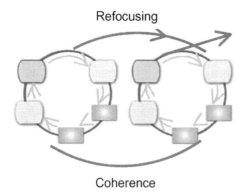

Refocusing

Coherence

Throughout this book I have promoted the idea that the purpose of professional learning is to develop the professionalism of teachers as adaptive experts who work in schools with high adaptive capacity. Keeping it all going, therefore, should not be seen as some kind of survival test for teachers and the leaders of the schools in which they work as they try to maintain new practices in an area of focus. Rather, keeping it all going is about making the processes underpinning the cycles of inquiry and knowledge-building core business for the professionals responsible for students' learning. The reason for this framing is that the evidence points to its veracity. Although the research base is relatively recent, and still developing, ongoing gains in outcomes for students are more evident in professional learning initiatives that develop adaptive expertise than those that do not.[92]

The issue of keeping it all going is usually referred to in terms of sustainability. Debates around this contested term in education involve three dimensions. The first is whether sustainability is about maintenance or improvement.[93] Maintenance arguments are usually advanced in situations involving a short-term influx of resources, professional development opportunities and other forms of assistance, then withdrawn. The sustainability question becomes one of ascertaining if the injection of these resources leaves a footprint behind them. A position more consistent with the development of adaptive expertise is that sustainability requires the much tougher test of ongoing improvement. Adaptive expertise has within it deeply embedded notions of ongoing learning and improvement. Maintenance implies a satisfaction with the status quo with little more to be learned. Maintenance runs the danger of becoming stuck in a time warp. Sustainability is about ongoing improvement in student outcomes and professional practice.

The second dimension concerns the focus and measurement of that improvement. Does sustainability refer to changes in leadership and teaching practices? Should it focus on outcomes for students? If so, should these outcomes be restricted to those that are the focus of the professional learning or include outcomes beyond this focus? The answer consistent with notions of adaptive expertise is that sustainability encompasses all these dimensions. Students (their engagement, learning and well-being) are the touchstone at the centre of improvement efforts. Improvement in one kind of outcome for students is connected to improvements in others. Possible negative effects are monitored to ensure that improvement in one area does not result in problems in another.

Ongoing improvement in student outcomes is unlikely to happen, however, unless there are ongoing changes in teaching and leadership practices. Decisions about learning foci become embedded in iterative inquiry cycles that deepen knowledge over time about all aspects of the work of teaching and learning by teachers, leaders and those who facilitate their learning. Learning systems for students, teachers and leaders have an underlying coherence.

The third dimension asks whether sustainability means going it alone or seeking the support of others. Adaptive experts know the limitations of their expertise and when, and from where, to seek help when new challenges arise. They become interdependent with the wider education community to help them shape their improvement efforts. From this perspective, the distinction between learning something and sustaining it becomes blurred. It is not a case of learning then sustaining what is learned. Rather, it is a case of ongoing learning, being aware when a situation is so challenging that it means going back to basics, or when all it requires is to refocus what is already known. Sustainability requires developing interdependence with those with specific expertise.

Thus, the notions of developing systems for refocusing inquiry and deepening knowledge through iterative cycles, and broadening foci to compass new areas in ways that form a coherent learning system are central to sustaining ongoing improvement across students, teaching and leading.[94] I will elaborate these two ideas in the next section, then discuss implications for policy.

> "Notions of developing systems for refocusing inquiry and deepening knowledge through iterative cycles, and broadening foci to compass new areas in ways that form a coherent learning system are central to sustaining ongoing improvement across students, teaching and leading."

Iterative cycles of inquiry

Pam O'Connell[95] draws a distinction between recursive and iterative cycles of inquiry. Recursive cycles ask the same questions framed in the same way and may lead to deeper knowledge in a particular area. There comes a point, however, when it is necessary to employ different strategies to take the next step up in improving practice and outcomes for students. Strategies that were successful initially may not be the ones that take teaching and learning to a deeper level. Different groups of students may need to become the focus with new questions asked about them. For example, teachers working with the cycle over some time may have developed professional knowledge and practice sufficiently to address the learning needs of most underachieving students in mathematics. Taking another look at the assessment information may identify a group of learners who still are not making expected progress. Which particular mathematical concepts present difficulties for them? Is engagement the real problem? Do they feel safe to express their confusions in class? The specific needs of these students may become the next cycle's focus. In this way, the cycles move from being recursive to iterative. Adaptive experts differentiate their learning as they pinpoint new groups of students or new areas of learning and retest their assumptions about how best to approach the new challenge. The same principles apply and are illustrated in Figure 8.1.

Schools with high adaptive capacity develop the adaptive expertise of their

> "Schools with high adaptive capacity develop the adaptive expertise of their teachers as they help them to construct and reconstruct their environments through cycles of inquiry and knowledge-building to meet student needs better."

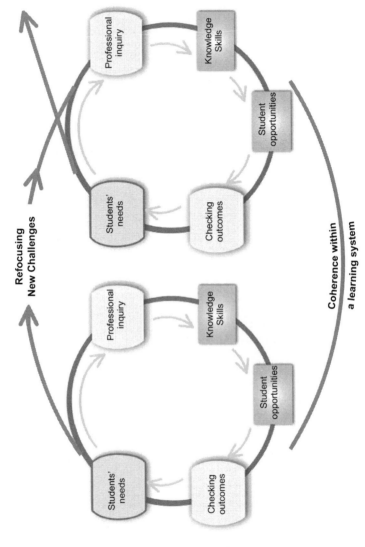

Figure 8.1 Keeping it all going through coherence of inquiry

teachers as they help them to construct and reconstruct their environments through iterative cycles of inquiry and knowledge-building to meet student needs better. A number of cases have been described throughout this book illustrating these deepening cycles, such as the teachers who examined their contribution to the drop in achievement over the summer. A feature of many of these schools, particularly those facing challenging circumstances, is that they treat such circumstances as problems to be solved rather than as reasons to explain why they cannot be more effective.[96]

All approaches to sustainability have within them an assumption that the practices or outcomes in need of being sustained must become part of the schools' organizational routines. From the perspective of the adaptive expert, the most important routines are the processes underpinning the inquiry and knowledge-building cycles, with systems, structures and personnel supporting the cycles to become core school business. Systems may include the regular review of student assessment information for its implications for teaching and leadership practices. Structures might involve regular team meetings to examine student work or to bring newly identified problems of teaching and learning for collective discussion.

Developing personnel may mean the promoting of leadership expertise to lead these discussions. One of the cases described in Chapter 5 illustrated how one principal developed the leadership expertise of her deputy to run the newly introduced monitoring meetings to examine progress in student learning. Developing leadership capacity was an integral part of promoting professional learning throughout this school.

One of the threats to these kinds of practices becoming core business lies in the ways in which roles and responsibilities are structured in schools. It is tempting to say that teachers make the greatest difference to student learning, so that those with specialist expertise should work directly with the teachers to improve their capability. Indeed, this approach might result in short-term gains but is unlikely to result in sustainable gains across the school as an organization if it usurps the legitimate role of the leaders as leaders of learning. Adaptive capacity of the school as an organization is not developed through bypassing the learning needs of leaders. While it may be appropriate at times for specialist experts to work directly with teachers, sustainability depends on the extent to which leadership capability to undertake this role is developed within the school. When the main thrust of any intervention is with leaders, they become lead learners who learn how to develop the adaptive expertise of their teachers.

Creating coherence

So far, much of my discussion of the cycles of inquiry has involved going deeper in an area of focus to solve new problems as they arise with different groups of students. Staying within these boundaries, however, can become as much of a time warp as a maintenance notion of sustainability. The purpose for engaging in deep inquiry within a single focus must be to understand the processes in sufficient depth so that they can be applied beyond this focus. Innovation within schools, across schools and local authorities requires much broader notions of inquiry. It is here that coherence among inquiry foci comes into play.

The importance of coherence in making a difference to students' achievement became prominent with the work of Fred Newman and colleagues[97] in Chicago where they identified that those schools focusing on fewer co-ordinated programmes of instruction undertaken over a sustained period of time showed greater improvement in achievement than others. Their image of the alternative in which schools take on initiatives and programmes like plucking presents off a Christmas tree has endured because this is what so many schools do. They are more likely to do this when facing difficult circumstances and a requirement to do something about them.

Coherence has many dimensions that in essence means maintaining consistency across different foci so innovations hang together. My focus in this book and chapter is coherence within professional learning and its sustainability – coherence as a learning system and coherence of adaptations to teaching practices.

Coherence as a learning system

The idea of coherence can conjure up images of alignment with everything looking the same. Thus, it becomes an idea to be rejected because of its stultifying potential. Coherence as a learning system, in fact, requires high levels of energy and innovation with students' engagement, learning and well-being as the touchstone.

Coherence within this context also means that new areas of learning and inquiry are linked to previous areas of inquiry. When thinking about what next, consideration is given to what has been learned before. The main purpose of linking areas is to facilitate the transfer of key ideas from one focus to another. For example, if teachers are learning about formative assessment in reading, then understanding how formative assessment might be used in the social sciences can speed up the transfer of important ideas. What was learned about social interactions with students in one situation is related to another. Examining what applies across all curriculum

> "Students are the reason for professionals to engage in learning and success in developing better engagement, learning and well-being is the mark of success of any intervention or innovation."

areas and situations and what is unique to each develops this understanding. Under these circumstances, both teachers and students are more likely to recognize and apply their previous learning. This kind of coherence requires a whole school strategic approach to professional learning. Professional learning plans come to mirror student learning plans with both tied to strategic goals for the school as an organization. This does not mean that professional learning plans look the same for everyone. It means that they all pull in the same direction.

Given that problems in different areas usually introduce new challenges, linking areas of inquiry can result in the realization that previous understandings need to be revisited. Through working with formative assessment principles in the social sciences, for example, teachers may come to realize that they did not fully understand important ideas about formative assessment in an earlier language context. The purpose of linking the inquiries is to deepen understandings in both familiar and unfamiliar areas.

Coherence as a learning system also means that approaches to professional and student learning are consistent with the principles underpinning the inquiry and knowledge-building cycle. To inquire into students' learning needs and one's own learning needs as a professional, only to be confronted with a set of scripted lessons for either themselves or their students, would be antithetical to the values of professionalism promoted in this book and the research on how people learn.

Coherence of adaptations to teaching practices

In any professional learning situation, teachers adapt what is learned to their particular contexts. Professional learning facilitators sometimes see these adaptations as problems with implementation. This thinking is summed up in the expression of frustration I have sometimes heard, 'If only teachers would do what they have been taught!' In reality, if they wish teachers to become responsive to students, then adaptations should be expected. Problems arise when adaptations are dictated by prior conceptions about what is effective, and those prior conceptions are inconsistent with the principles underpinning new practices promoted through professional learning. The problem becomes even greater when the adaptations are assumed to be effective and not examined for their effectiveness.

Achieving coherence in adaptations to practice means, therefore, that the adaptations are consistent with the theory of the new approach and lead to improved student learning. In the following case, I decribe how adaptations varied in a study I undertook in seven schools and the consequences for achievement.

'We need to learn how to do it better.'[98]

(Teacher)

In this study the teachers of kindergarten-aged students had all participated in six months of intensive professional learning. The schools were located in communities with few financial resources. The students in two of the schools made greater gains than in the other five in the year following their involvement in the professional development. When asked what they had adapted over this time, teachers in all the schools indicated they had made some changes to their practice. In the five schools whose students made slower progress, the teachers all justified their adaptations in terms of meeting students' needs more effectively. The achievement profiles of the students contradicted their assumptions. On closer inspection the adaptations involved making new practice more consistent with previous familiar practice.

The teachers in the two schools with higher gains made fewer adaptations. They monitored student learning closely and when faced with a learning problem they were unable to solve, the leaders in these schools sought the advice of the external expert who had worked with them during the initial six months to develop solutions consistent with the principles of the new approach. Through this process they deepened their knowledge in ways that could be used for all students. The teachers in these two schools constantly talked about their need to learn how to teach better by understanding the approach in greater depth.

Inquiry, coherence and policy

I began this book with expressions of disappointment from a range of groups, including those in policy roles, about the limitations of teacher professional development in achieving policy goals of raising the bar and closing the gap. Clearly, in many situations the policy intent has not been realized. Jim Spillane[99] suggests that the reason for many of these kinds of problems lies in the interpretive space between policy intent and teachers' existing knowledge and understandings as they attempt to make sense of the policy messages. The central theme of this book is that activities in this interpretive space must be constructed specifically to promote learning through the system layers. This learning needs to be reciprocal and involve both practitioners' understanding of the policy and the understanding of those responsible for the policy from the practitioners' perspective. Policy officials need to learn about the efficacy of the policies themselves and why they are being implemented in particular ways.

I am not the first to suggest that it is imperative for policy to become part of a learning system with policy officials also engaging in systematic and deliberate professional learning about the effectiveness of their professional activities.[100] Their influence in the system is central to professional learning and its sustainability. Just as teachers cannot be expected to solve the urgent problems facing schools and the education system without the learning and support of their leaders, school leaders and teachers cannot be expected to solve the problems of the system without the learning and support of those responsible for developing policy, deciding on funding priorities and providing leadership within the education system.

The best evidence synthesis on professional learning and development identified that the policy environments in which schools operate make a difference. In many cases policy officials at the district or national levels promoted high-quality professional learning through providing relevant learning opportunities and appropriate levels of funding that had conditions for sustainability built into them. In some other situations, the policy environment reduced schools' effectiveness by creating conflicting policy demands, taking approaches to professional learning that were inconsistent with how people learn and withdrawing funding just as the learning was gaining traction. Possibly more has been written on the latter situation than the former.[101] Part of the reason is that policy officials do not always have control of the content of professional learning policies or the funding available. At times they may even be required to implement policies that contradict the conditions for quality professional learning. But in many cases they do have influence, if not a great deal of control, and I want to draw attention to possibilities for developing policies consistent with a view of teachers as adaptive experts who work in schools with high adaptive capacity because these are essential to effective implementation and to sustainability.

Policy and inquiry

I have promoted the idea throughout this book that teachers, leaders and facilitators of professional learning must know 'their class' in all its diversity if they are to be successful in promoting student, teacher and leader learning. Policy officials have classes that are even more complex and diverse than others but nowhere in the system is it more important to know one's class. Without this knowledge, the most likely outcome is for policy officials to be left wondering why the implementation of their carefully developed policies does not resemble what was intended and does not have the desired impact. Much of the reason for the success of the literacy professional development project in New Zealand that led to sustained improvement in students' literacy achievement as described in Chapter 1 is the approach taken by policy officials in the Ministry of Education who were responsible for its development. Evidence-informed inquiry was central to the policy approach as described in the following case.

'We needed to unpack the layers.'[102]

(Policy official responsible for professional development)

The evidence from international literacy surveys showed that New Zealand has a high-quality, low equity system. Although students achieve well on average, a significant number do not do so. This latter group became the main focus of the literacy professional development project. The premises of the project were formulated using available research into effective literacy practices for the groups of students not achieving well and consultation with recognized experts in the field. The private organization that won the contract to provide the professional support services to schools was required to provide evidence of improvement in students' literacy achievement, evidence of effective in-school professional communities, and evidence of building teachers' knowledge and practice.

An emphasis on inquiry throughout the project was implied in the ministry statements about the approach underpinning it. One described the goals as, 'We want everyone involved to be clear about their own learning needs, to receive quality information about them and to be involved in relevant decisions about how they can support [student] learners.'

Consistent with these values was the kind of evidence the ministry sought throughout the life of the project. Each year the ministry, external researchers and professional learning providers decided on the focus for independent research and within-project monitoring. The ministry's focus was always on who was learning what and how the broad strategy was being translated into practice. The ministry leaders were open to what they needed to learn. In response to the research into the layers of student, teacher, leader and facilitator learning, one ministry official described her understanding as an early breakthrough, 'We were very much thinking about the student as the outcome without being able to unpack it ... it's like peeling back the layers.'

Regular milestone reports moved from traditional forms of accountability for inputs and money spent to an evidence-informed inquiry. The process began with the evidence related to outcomes in the initial contract at student, teacher and school levels. A combination of oral and formal written conversations followed culminating in a revised report that identified what had been learned, what had worked well, what more needed to be found out and what needed to be changed in both the project and policy approach.

An example of learning by policy officials came relatively early in the project. Strong emphasis was placed on unpacking students' profiles of achievement to find out who was benefiting and who was not. Although students in the lowest 20 per cent of the distribution showed greater gains in achievement than others, further examination of the data identified a core of students at the very bottom who had not made much progress. A number of policy responses were considered, including refocusing the project on these students. After lengthy discussion with the professional learning facilitators and school leaders, it was decided that these students needed specialist intervention that went beyond reasonable expectations of regular classroom teachers. The policy response was to ask facilitators to work with school leaders to ensure that specialist resources within the school were focused on meeting the needs of these students.

These policy officials regarded their class as the different layers of the system and constructed probes through the research and project reports to investigate understanding and learning at each layer. The question was not about faithful implementation of the policy but about what their classes were learning and how they could be supported. The policy officials, in turn, were open to learning about making adjustments to the policy and its implementation. Professional learning for themselves or for others in the system, however, was not enough. The focus of the professional learning had to meet the ultimate contracted outcome of promoting student learning. This requirement was the hard edge to the policy. Student learning on both the surface and deeper features of literacy were closely monitored and the difficulties that arose were accompanied by conversations consistent with the properties in Figure 2.1 of relevant evidence, inquiry habits of mind, relationships of respect and challenge and accessing relevant expertise. Relevant evidence, usually from the milestone reporting processes and the accompanying independent research formed the basis of the conversations. Inquiry habits of mind were symbolized in the labelling of the project as 'an inquiry project' by the providers with project processes consistent with this label. Relationships of respect and challenge were evident in many ways, one of which was the change described to the process of milestone reporting in the case above. Expertise was constantly sought from independent researchers and literacy experts both inside and outside the project.[103]

Policy and coherence

Pam O'Connell[104] notes in her study of sustainability that actions of national or local authorities with responsibility for policy are usually discussed in terms of the threat they present to coherence and sustainability rather than how they support them. New system leaders are appointed with new visions. Mandates arrive on the desks of school leaders to take new directions. They require schools to respond. Such environments prevent sustainable learning systems and undermine coherence.

If policy officials want greater traction for their policies they need to consider how new directions for policy cohere with previous professional learning activities directed towards achieving earlier strategic priorities. The policy problem of education systems creating too many ad hoc, disconnected and superficial innovations has long been recognized, yet systems continue to do this. In his book on sustainability, Michael Fullan[105] talks about education systems 'connecting the dots'. The dots need to be connected vertically in terms of filling in the interpretive spaces between system layers, horizontally to develop collective understandings and across time to ensure sustainability.

A major threat to coherence and sustainability is having too many goals. When Ben Levin[106] described a recent approach to reform in Ontario, Canada, he emphasized the importance of a few coherent strategic goals rather than diverting efforts by having too many. In Ontario these goals included improving outcomes, reducing disparities and improving public confidence in education. Each education system faces its own challenges and needs to develop goals according to local priorities and needs. When they do so, a major consideration must be to establish coherence among the goals themselves with a focus on providing professional learning opportunities to build the capacity to achieve them. Ongoing decisions must be considered in terms of how they contribute to rather than detract from their accomplishment and sustainability.

All education systems are faced with overwhelming possibilities for priorities that compete for space and air time. As Ben Levin points out, it is hard to stay focused given the myriad demands. I argue that staying focused is both one of the greatest challenges and the greatest opportunities for policy officials to become system leaders that develop adaptive capacity throughout the system in ways that lead to sustainability. The distraction of multiple demands must be managed or coherence is inevitably sacrificed, as is the power of deep professional learning to contribute to ongoing system and school learning in the interests of students.

Conclusions

Realizing the power of professional learning to bring about the system lift to which many educational jurisdictions aspire can not be a command, control and support strategy.[107] Teaching and learning about teaching are more complex than this. Raising the bar and closing the gap requires a number of shifts in thinking and practice from traditional approaches to professional development. These shifts were identified in the introduction to this book and have been elaborated throughout. They include shifting:

- from participation in professional development to engagement in professional learning
- from focusing on teachers to ensuring students are at the centre of the process
- from foregrounding delivery methods to foregrounding professional knowledge and skills
- from focusing on theory or practice to meeting the double demand of theory and practice
- from teachers being a recipient of someone else's knowledge to becoming self-regulated learners
- from school leaders organizing professional learning to taking a leadership role for learning within their schools
- from policy officials seeing their role as providing learning opportunities for others to including their own learning in the process.

Much more than a list of bullet points is required for these shifts to have meaning. They involve shifts in thinking as much as shifts in focus and activity. They are underpinned by a theory of what it means to be professional and the kind of organizations and systems in which this professionalism is developed. In this final section I review the central ideas developed throughout the book about these underlying theories.

Professionals as adaptive experts

The approach to professional learning developed in this book is based on a view of professionalism encompassed in the idea of the adaptive expert. The 'expert' part of the descriptor means that learning opportunities for students are based on deep pedagogical content and assessment knowledge. This expertise is developed through professional learning becoming ongoing core business. The 'adaptive' part of the descriptor means that professionals not only use this knowledge to solve new problems but also to monitor when it is inadequate and different foci for professional learning are needed. Student progress is constantly reviewed for the implications for that teacher's teaching and learning, not for labelling students as successes and failures. Part of their expertise is to know when and from where to seek help. Adaptive experts are disciplined innovators who monitor their effectiveness in terms of the engagement, learning and well-being of all students in their care.

Schools with adaptive capacity

The environments in which teachers and others in the system teach strongly influence what and how they learn. Schools with high organizational adaptive capacity are more likely to develop teachers with adaptive expertise than those that do not. These schools have structures and routines designed to promote the learning of both individual professionals and of the school as a whole to better meet the needs of all students. Professional learning is at the core of the school's business. It is not an option to create patches of brilliance for the students of willing teachers and something less desirable for the students of the unwilling. When current knowledge and skills are insufficient to solve teaching and learning problems to meet the needs of all students, leaders ensure specific expertise is brought to bear. Leaders recognize they have as much or more to learn as their teachers to become effective leaders of learning. In schools with high adaptive capacity attention is given to how the school becomes a coherent learning system. Adaptations to practice are examined for their underlying coherence with what is known to be effective and checked for the kind of learning promoted. When moving to new innovations previous understandings are revisited to see what understandings can be transferred to new areas. Professional learning plans build on one another.

Systems with adaptive capacity

Systems that develop adaptive capacity have within them learning through the system layers. At all layers, including that of system leaders, adaptive expertise is evident in the way the professionals involved go about their professional activities. System leaders do not see professional development as something they provide for others. They see professional learning as being as focused on their learning about the quality of the opportunities provided throughout the system to develop organizational and professional adaptive expertise. When they assess their effectiveness, students' engagement, learning and well-being form the touchstone of system activities. Systems with high adaptive capacity have a few important strategic goals that are coherent with one another. The dots are connected through the system layers, across the layers and over time.

The power of professional learning

The evidence from the research underpinning this book indicates that the power of professional learning can be realized. There are sufficient examples in which leaders' and teachers' engagement in such learning has made a substantive difference to students, particularly for those who are not well served by our education systems. While I readily acknowledge that education cannot fix the problems of society alone and that many children live in circumstances that make it challenging for them to learn, there is no professional justification for the persistence of such wide disparities in students' profiles of achievement that currently exist. To change these profiles will require the collective will of the educators at all levels of the system to change how we approach the task of promoting the learning of all.

Notes

Chapter 1: From Professional Development to Professional Learning

1 Sparks, D. (2004) Focusing staff development on improving the learning of all students, in G. Cawelti (ed) *Handbook of Research on Improving Student Achievement* (3rd edn, p. 247). Arlington, VA: Educational Research Service.

2 Cuban, L. (1994) *How Teachers Taught: Constancy and Change in American Classrooms 1890–1980*, p. 2. New York: Teachers College Press.

3 For example, see Correnti, R. (2007) An empirical investigation of professional development effects on literacy instruction using daily logs, *Educational Evaluation and Policy Analysis,* 29(4): 262–95.

4 Hanushek, E. (2005) Economic outcomes and school quality. Education Policy Series. International Academy of Education and International Institute for Educational Planning, UNESCO. Available online at/www. smec.curtin.edu.au/iae/, p. 19.

5 Timperley, H., Wilson, A., Barrar, H. and Fung, I. (2008) Best Evidence Synthesis on Professional Learning and Development. Report to the Ministry of Education, Wellington, New Zealand.

6 Timperley, H., Parr, J. and Meissel, K. (2010) Making a difference to student achievement in literacy. Final Research Report on the Literacy Professional Development Project. Wellington: Learning Media Ltd.

7 O'Connell, P., Timperley, H., Parr, J. and Meissel, K. (2008) Is sustainability of educational reform an article of faith or can it be deliberately crafted? Paper presented at the British Educational Research Association Conference, Edinburgh, 3–6 September.

8 Guskey, T.R. (2000) *Evaluating Professional Development*. Thousand Oaks, CA: Corwin Press.

9 Kaser, L. and Halbert, J. (2009) *Leadership Mindsets: Innovation and Learning in the Transformation of Schools*. London and New York: Routledge.

10 Doyle, W. (1990) Themes in teacher education research, in W. Houston (ed) *Handbook of Research on Teacher Education*. New York: Macmillan.

11 Fullan, M. (2005) *Leadership Sustainability: System Thinkers in Action*. Thousand Oaks, CA: Corwin Press.

12 Hatano, G. and Oura, Y. (2003) Commentary: reconceptualizing school learning using insight from expertise research, *Educational Researcher*, 32: 26–29.

13 Hammerness, K., Darling-Hammond, L., Bransford, J., Berliner, D., Cochran-Smith, M., McDonald, M. and Zeichner, K. (2005) How teachers learn and develop, in L. Darling-Hammond (ed) *Preparing Teachers for a Changing World: What Teachers Should Learn and Be Able to Do* (pp. 358–89). San Francisco, CA: John Wiley & Sons.

14 Putnam, R.T. and Borko, H. (2000) What do new views of knowledge and thinking have to say about research on teacher learning? *Educational Researcher*, 29(1): 4–15.

15 A number of studies have observed that teachers have the greatest system influence on student outcomes, for example: Cuttance, P. (1998) Quality assurance reviews as a catalyst for school improvement in Australia, in A. Hargreaves, A. Lieberman, M. Fullan and D. Hopkins (eds) *International Handbook of Educational Change* (Part 2: pp.1135–62). Dordrecht, Netherlands: Kluwer Publishers.

   Muijs, D. and Reynolds, D. (2001) *Effective Teaching: Evidence and Practice*. London: Paul Chapman Publishing.

   Nye, B., Konstantanopoulos, S. and Hedges, L.V. (2004) How large are teacher effects? *Educational Evaluation and Policy Analysis,* 26(3): 237–57.

16 Bransford, J., Derry, S., Berliner, D. and Hammerness, K. (2005) Theories of learning and their roles in teaching, in L. Darling-Hammond and J. Bransford (eds) *Preparing Teachers for a Changing World* (pp. 40–87). San Francisco, CA: John Wiley & Sons.

17 Robinson, V.M.J., Lloyd, C. and Rowe, K.J. (2008) The impact of leadership on student outcomes: an analysis of the differential effects of leadership type, *Educational Administration Quarterly*, 44(5): 635–74.

18 Kaser and Halbert, 2009. *See* note 9.

Chapter 2: Finding Out About Students

19 Hammerness, K. et al. (2005) How teachers learn and develop, in L. Darling-Hammond (ed) *Preparing Teachers for a Changing World: What Teachers Should Learn and Be Able to Do* (pp. 358–89). San Francisco, CA: John Wiley & Sons.

20 Bransford, J., Brown, A. and Cocking, R. (2000) *How People Learn: Brain, Mind, Experience and School.* Washington, DC: National Academy Press.

21 Donovan, M.S., Bransford, J.D. and Pellegrino, J.W. (eds) (1999) *How People Learn: Bridging Research and Practice.* Washington, DC: National Academy Press. The original reads: 'Students come to classrooms with pre-conceptions about how the world works. If their initial understandings is not engaged, they may fail to grasp the new concepts and information that are taught, or they may learn them for the purposes of a test but revert to their preconceptions outside the classroom' (p. 20).

22 Butler, R. (1987) Enhancing and undermining intrinsic motivation: the effects of task-involving and ego-involving evaluation on interest and performance, *British Journal of Educational Psychology*, 58: 1–14.

23 This example is based on the work of Mei Lai and Stuart McNaughton who work in a research and development role with schools in New Zealand.

24 Lai, M., McNaughton, S., Timperley, H. and Hsiao, S. (2009) Sustaining continued acceleration in reading comprehension achievement following an intervention, *Educational Assessment, Evaluation and Accountability*, 1(1): 81–100.

25 This case is adapted from the research reported in Lai, McNaughton, Timperley and Hsiao, 2009. *See* note 24.

26 Earl, L. and Timperley, H. (2008) *Professional Learning Conversations: Challenges in Using Evidence for Improvement.* London: Springer Academic Publishers.

27 A number of studies have demonstrated the importance of teacher influence including the following:

Nye, B., Konstantanopoulos, S. and Hedges, L.V. (2004) How large are teacher effects? *Educational Evaluation and Policy Analysis,* 26(3): 237–57.

Cuttance, P. (1998) Quality assurance reviews as a catalyst for school improvement in Australia, in A. Hargreaves, A. Lieberman, M. Fullan and D. Hopkins (eds) *International Handbook of Educational Change* (Part 2: pp. 1135–62). Dordrecht, Netherlands: Kluwer Publishers.

Muijs, D. and Reynolds, D. (2001) *Effective Teaching: Evidence and Practice.* London: Paul Chapman Publishing.

28   Dall'Alba, G. and Sandberg, J. (2006) Unveiling professional development: a critical review of stage models, *Review of Educational Research,* 76(3): 383–403.

Chapter 3: Building Teacher Knowledge

29   Black, P. and Wiliam, D. (1998) Assessment and classroom learning, *Assessment in Education,* 5(1): 7–75.
30   Elmore, R. (2004) *School Reform from the Inside Out: Policy, Practice and Performance.* Cambridge, MA: Harvard Education Press.
31   Wilson, S. and Berne, J. (1999) Teacher learning and the acquisition of professional knowledge: an examination of research on contemporary professional development, in A. Iran-Nejad and P.D. Pearson (eds) *Review of Research in Education* (Vol. 24, pp. 173–210). Washington, DC: AERA.
32   Timperley, H., Wilson, A., Barrar, H. and Fung, I. (2008) Best evidence synthesis on professional learning and development. Report to the Ministry of Education, Wellington, New Zealand.
33   Timperley, H.S., Parr, J.M. and Bertanees, C. (2009) Promoting professional inquiry for improved outcomes for students in New Zealand, *Professional Development in Education,* 35(2): 227–45.
34   Coburn, C.E. (2001) Collective sensemaking about reading: how teachers mediate reading policy in their professional communities, *Educational Evaluation and Policy Analysis,* 23(2): 145–70.
35   Bransford, Brown and Cocking, 2000. *See* note 20.
36   Putman and Borko, 2000. *See* note 14.
37   Shulman, L.S. (1987) Knowledge and teaching: foundations of the new reform, *Harvard Educational Review,* 57(1): 1–22.

38 Parr, J.M. and Timperley, H.S. (2010) Feedback to writing, assessment for teaching and learning and student progress, *Assessing Writing*, 15: 65–85.

39 Black and Wiliam, 1998. *See* note 29.

40 Earl, L. (2003) *Assessment as Learning: Using Classroom Assessment to Maximize Student Learning*. Thousand Oaks, CA: Corwin Press.

41 Bransford, Brown and Cocking, 2000. *See* note 20.

42 Lucas, B. and Claxton, G. (2010) *New Kinds of Smart: How the Science of Learnable Intelligence is Changing Education*. Maidenhead: Open University Press.

43 Dany, G. (2009) A Reflection on Helen Timperley's Teacher Professional Learning and Development, Concept paper, Vancouver Island University.

44 This description was developed through interviews with the principal and staff of a special school in London, England.

Chapter 4: Checking New Opportunities for Students

45 Black and Wiliam, 1998. *See* note 29.

46 Le Fevre, D. (2010) Changing tack: professional learning as a process of change, in H. Timperley and J. Parr (eds) *Weaving Evidence, Inquiry and Standards to Build Better Schools* (pp. 71–92). Wellington, New Zealand: New Zealand Council for Educational Research.

47 Bransford, Brown and Cocking, 2000. *See* note 20.

48 Alton-Lee, A., Nuthal, G. and Patrick, J. (1993) Reframing classroom research: a lesson from the private world of children, *Harvard Educational Review*, 63(1): 50–84.

49 Timperley, H.S. (2005) Distributed leadership: developing theory from practice, *Journal of Curriculum Studies*, 37(6): 395–420.

50 Timperley, 2005. Ibid.

51 Timperley, 2005. Ibid.

52 Hatano, G. and Inagaki, K. (1986) Two courses of expertise, in H. Stevenson, H. Azama and K. Hakuta (eds) *Child Development and Education in Japan* (pp. 262–72). New York: Freeman.

53 Bransford, Derry, Berliner, and Hammerness (2005) *See* note 16. Theories of learning and their roles in teaching, in L. Darling-Hammond and J. Bransford (eds) *Preparing Teachers for a Changing World* (pp. 40–87). San Francisco, CA: John Wiley & Sons.

Chapter 5: School Leaders as Leaders of Learning

54 Elmore, 2004. *See* note 30.
55 Robinson, V., Höhepa, M. and Lloyd, C. (2009) *School Leadership and Student Outcomes: Identifying What Works and Why: A Best Evidence Synthesis.* Wellington: Ministry of Education.
56 For example, Stein, M. and Nelson, B. (2003) Leadership content knowledge, *Educational Evaluation and Policy Analysis,* 25: 423–48.
57 Kaser and Halbert, 2009. *See* note 9.
58 Spillane, J.P., Halverson, R. and Diamond, J. (2004) Towards a theory of leadership practice: a distributed perspective, *Journal of Curriculum Studies,* 36(1): 3–34.
59 Timperley, H. (in press) Knowledge and the leadership of professional learning, *Leadership and Policy in Schools.*
60 Earl, L. and Hannay, L. (2011) Educational leaders as knowledge workers, in J. Robertson and H. Timperley (eds) *Leadership and Learning.* London: Sage Publications.
61 Timperley, H. and Hulsbosch, N. (2010) Instructional leadership in action. Paper presented to the American Educational Research Association Annual Meeting, Denver, Colorado, April.
62 Robinson, Höhepa and Lloyd, 2009. *See* note 55.
63 Earl, L. and Katz, S. (2006) *Leading in a Data Rich World.* Thousand Oaks, CA: Corwin Press.
64 Kaser and Halbert, 2009. *See* note 9.
65 Bryk, A. and Schneider, B. (2002) *Trust in Schools: A Core Resource for Improvement.* New York: Russell Sage Foundation Publications, and Bryk, A., Sebring, P., Allensworth, E. and Luppescu, S. (2010) *Organizing Schools for Improvement: Lessons from Chicago.* Chicago, IL: University of Chicago Press.
66 Staber, U. and Sydow, J. (2002) Organizational adaptive capacity: a structuration perspective, *Journal of Management Inquiry,* 11(4): 408–24.

Chapter 6: Bringing the Parts of the Cycle Together

67 Spillane, Halverson and Diamond, 2004. *See* note 58.
68 Bransford, Brown and Cocking, 2000. *See* note 20.
69 Stoll, L. (2011) Leading professional learning communities, in J. Robertson and H. Timperley (eds) *Leadership and Learning* (pp. 101–17). London: Sage Publications.

70 Stoll, L., Fink, D. and Earl, L. (2003) *It's About Learning [and It's About Time]: What is in it for Schools?* (p. 131) London: RoutledgeFalmer.
71 Stoll, 2011. *See* note 70.
72 Stoll, L., Halbert, J. and Kaser, L. (2011) Deepening learning in school-to-school networks, in C. Day (ed) *International Handbook on Teacher and School Development*. London: Routledge.
73 The, then, Qualifications and Curriculum Authority, introduced personal learning and thinking skills within the new National Curriculum for secondary schools in September 2008.
74 Cooperrider, D.L. and Srivastva, S. (1987) Appreciative inquiry in organizational life, in W. Pasmore and R. Woodman (eds) *Research in Organization Change and Development* (Vol. 1). Greenwich, CT: JAI Press.
75 GCSEs are the final statutory examinations taken in England at age 16 and A Levels are examinations taken two years later, usally by students aiming to go on into higher education.
76 Stoll, 2011. *See* note 70.
77 L'Allier, S., Elish-Piper, L. and Bean, R. (2010) *What Matters for Elementary Literacy Coaching? Guiding Principles for Instructional Improvement and Student Achievement* (2nd edn). Newark, DE: International Reading Association.
78 Bransford, Brown and Cocking, 2000. *See* note 20.
79 Parr, J. and Timperley, H. (2009) Literacy Professional Development Project (2008). Report to the Ministry of Education. Wellington, New Zealand.

Chapter 7: Some Challenges in Facilitating Professional Learning

80 Wilson and Berne, 1999. *See* note 31.
81 Hammerness, K., et al. (2005) *See* note 13. How teachers learn and develop, in L. Darling-Hammond (ed) *Preparing Teachers for a Changing World: What Teachers should Learn and be Able to do* (pp. 358–89). San Francisco, CA: John Wiley & Sons.
82 Bishop, R., Berryman, M., Powell, A. and Teddy, L. (2005) *Te Kotahitanga: Improving the Educational Achievement of Māori Students in Mainstream Education. Phase 2: Towards a Whole School Approach* (Progress report and planning document). Wellington: Ministry of Education.
83 Robinson, Lloyd, and Rowe (2008). *See* note 17. The impact of leadership on student outcomes: an analysis of the differential effects

of leadership type, *Educational Administration Quarterly,* 44(5): 635–74.

84 Timperley, H. and Parr, J. (2009) Chain of influence from policy to practice in the New Zealand literacy strategy, *Research Papers in Education,* 24(2): 135–54.

85 Timperley and Parr, 2009. *See* note 84.

86 Timperley, Parr and Meissel, 2010. *See* note 6.

87 Robinson, V. and Walker, J. (1999) Theoretical privilege and researchers' contribution to educational change, in J.S. Gaffney and B.J. Askew (eds) *Stirring the Waters: The Influence of Marie Clay* (pp. 349–81). Portsmouth, NH: Heinemann.

88 Bransford, Brown and Cocking, 2000. *See* note 20.

89 For example, Dreyfus, H. and Dreyfus, S. (1986) *Mind Over Machine: The Power of Human Intuition and Expertise in the Era of the Computer.* New York: Free Press.

90 Wang, J. and Odell, S. (2002) Mentored learning to teach according to standards-based reform: a critical review, *Review of Educational Research,* 72(3): 481–546.

91 See, for example, Van der Sijde, P. (1989) The effect of a brief teacher training on student achievement, *Teaching and Teacher Education,* 5(4): 303–14.

Kerman, S., Kimball, T. and Martin, M. (1980) *Teacher Expectations and Student Achievement: Coordinator Manual.* Bloomington, IN: Phi Delta Kappa.

Chapter 8: Keeping It All Going

92 Three recent works that have included notions of adaptive expertise within sustainability include:

Knight, N. (2009) Sustaining improved student outcomes and teaching practice in mathematics. Unpublished Ph.D. thesis, The University of Auckland.

Lai, M., McNaughton, S., Timperley, H. and Hsiao, S. (2009) Sustaining continued acceleration in reading comprehension achievement following an intervention, *Educational Assessment, Evaluation and Accountability,* 1(1), 81–100.

O'Connell, P. (2009) Is sustainability of schooling improvement an article of faith or can it be deliberately crafted? Unpublished Ph.D. thesis, The University of Auckland.

93 While few writers on sustainability refer to a notion of strict adherence to programme fidelity within their definitions, some research designs have an implicit assumption that sustainability is about implementation fidelity. More often maintenance views are expressed in terms of adaptations consistent with programme principles. See, for example, Century, J.R. and Levy, A.J. (2002) Sustaining change: a study of nine school districts with enduring programs. Paper presented at the the Annual Meeting of the American Educational Research Association, New Orleans, LA. Other works discussed in this chapter have assumptions of improvement within their definitions.

94 The two works by Lai et al. (2009) and O'Connell (2009) both have dimensions of inquiry and coherence in their conceptualization of sustainability.

95 O'Connell, 2009. *See* note 92.

96 Lai et al., 2009. *See* note 24.

97 Newmann, F.M., Smith, B.A., Allensworth, E. and Bryk, T. (2001) Instructional program coherence: what it is and why it should guide school improvement policy, *Educational Evaluation and Policy Analysis,* 23(4): 297–321.

98 Timperley, H.S. (2005) Distributed leadership: developing theory from practice, *Journal of Curriculum Studies,* 37(6): 395–420.

99 Spillane, J.P. (2004) *Standards Deviation: How Schools Misunderstand Education Policy.* Cambridge, MA: Harvard University Press.

100 Fullan, 2005. *See* note 11.

101 Several authors have critiqued the contribution of policy decisions in reducing the positive effects of professional learning. See, for example:

Coburn, C., Touré, J. and Yamashita, M. (2009) Evidence, interpretation and persuasion: instructional decision making at the district central office, *Teachers College Record,* 111(4): 1115–16.

Datnow, A. (2005) The sustainability of comprehensive reform models in changing district and state contexts, *Educational Administration Quarterly,* 41(1): 121–53.

102 Timperley and Parr, 2009. *See* note 84.

103 O'Connell, 2009. *See* note 92.

104 O'Connell, 2009. *See* note 92.

105 Fullan, 2005 (p. 22). *See* note 11.

106 Levin B. (2008) *How to Change 5000 Schools.* Cambridge, MA: Harvard Educational Press.

107 Fullan, 2005. *See* note 11.

Index

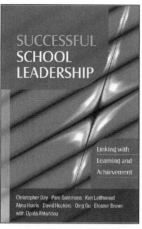

SUCCESSFUL SCHOOL LEADERSHIP
Linking with Learning and Achievement

Christopher Day, Pam Sammons, Ken Leithwood, David Hopkins, Qing Gu, Eleanor J. Brown & Elpida Ahtaridou

978-0-33524-243-6 (Paperback)
May 2011

eBook also available

This book provides a comprehensive analysis of the values and qualities of head teachers, the strategies they use and how they adapt these to their particular school context in order to ensure positive increases in the learning, well being and achievement of their students. The authors introduce the notions of 'layered leadership' and 'progressive trust' as key features of successful leadership.

Key Features of the text are:

- Illustrative case studies of successful primary and secondary headteachers' work
- Explores the particular differences as well as similarities in successful leadership behaviour between primary and secondary schools

www.openup.co.uk

 OPEN UNIVERSITY PRESS
McGraw - Hill Education

PROFESSIONAL LEARNING COMMUNITIES
Divergence, Depth and Dilemmas

Louise Stoll & Karen Seashore Louis

978-0-33522-030-4 (Paperback)
2007

This international collection expands perceptions and understanding of professional learning communities, as well as highlighting frequently neglected complexities and challenges. Drawing on research, each chapter offers a deeper understanding of topics, including:

- Distributed leadership
- Dialogue
- Organizational memory
- Trust
- Self-assessment and inquiry
- Purpose linked to learning

The last section of the book focuses upon three of the most challenging dilemmas that face developing professional learning communities:

- Developing professional learning communities in secondary school
- Building social capital
- Sustaining professional learning communities.

www.openup.co.uk